REINCARNATION & KARMA
Our Soul's Past-Life Influences

John Van Auken

Living in the Light
Virginia Beach, Virginia USA

Reincarnation & Karma

Initial Edition
Copyright © 1984 John Van Auken
Expanded Edition
Copyright © 2015 John Van Auken

An initial version was titled
*Born Again and Again:
How and Why Reincarnation Occurs*

JohnVanAuken.com
JohnVanAuken.newsletter@gmail.com

Living in the Light
P.O. Box 4942
Virginia Beach VA 23454 USA

Available from
Amazon.com, CreateSpace.com,
and other retail outlets

CONTENTS

Part One: The Fundamentals of Reincarnation
1. The Mysteries of Life — 9
2. Overlooked Messages in Genesis — 23
3. A Stellar Dimension — 39
4. The Physical Body — 45
5. To The Rescue! — 55
6. The Lives of Leila: One Soul's Journey — 67

Part Two: Reincarnation in Action
7. Past Lives & Present Relationships — 95
8. Destiny, Fate & Karma — 117
9. Past-Life Memory — 127
10. The Power of an Ideal — 149
11. Meditation — 155
12. Contact Dreams — 165

Part Three: Ancient Teachings
13. A Kabbalah View — 171
14. A Gnostic View — 181
15. A Hindu View — 185

A Note about Bible Quotes

Throughout this book the World English Bible (WEB) translation is used or, on occasion, the 1901 American Standard Version (ASV). These are used because their translations are copyright free. When using the American Standard Version, I have modernized the language, sentence structure, and syntax of this classic translation to better approximate the way we read and speak today. The World English Bible is in modern English.

A Note about Sources

Many of the sources for information in this book are ancient and classical historical records, such as the Bible, the *Rig Veda*, the Upanishads, *Bhagavad Gita*, Buddhist *Sutras*, the *Egyptian Book of the Dead*, the *Tibetan Book of the Dead*, the Mayan *Popol Vuh*, the Zoroastrian *Zend Avesta*, the Chinese, the Taoist *Secret of the Golden Flower*, and even some more current texts such as *The Aquarian Gospel* and *The Secret Teachings of All Ages*.

But there is also a source of information that is from the "Akashic Records." The *Akasha* is an ancient concept that has its origin in the oldest body of religious literature yet discovered in the world, the *Rig Veda*, circa 1300 BC, a collection of more than a thousand hymns written in an archaic form of Sanskrit, one of the oldest languages on Earth. The central myth in the *Rig Veda* is the myth of creation, told in several different ways. *Akasha* refers to the essence of life and the records of its activity since, during, and following the creation. It is a record that is recorded in the "ethers," not in stone or on parchment. It has been referred to as "The Book of Life" or "The Book of Remembrance." It may also be thought of as a collective mind upon which all the activities and thoughts of every individual mind make an impression, an impression that can be known or "read." The natural inclination to question such a source is understandable. Nevertheless, the content is included to give as full a picture of human knowledge on these topics as possible, leaving the reader to discern the value of this information.

This akashic source is the material from the American mystic Edgar Cayce (pronounced, KAY-see). These discourses were called "readings," because Cayce felt that he was reading the Book of Life or the Akashic Record. He was born on a farm near Hopkinsville, Kentucky, on March 18, 1877. As a child, he displayed unusual powers of perception. At the age of six, he told his parents that he could see "visions," sometimes of relatives who had recently died, sometimes of angels. He could also sleep with his head on his schoolbooks and awake with a photographic recall of their contents. Cayce would go into a hypnotic state to diagnose and prescribe healing for others, with so much success that doctors around Hopkinsville and Bowling Green took advantage of Cayce's unique talent to diagnose their patients. They soon discovered that all Cayce needed was the name and address of a patient to "tune in" telepathically to that individual's mind and body. The patient didn't have to be near Cayce, he could tune-in to them wherever they were. Eventually, Edgar Cayce, following advice from his own readings, moved to Virginia Beach, Virginia, and set up a hospital where he continued to conduct his "readings" for the health of others. But he also began a new line of readings called "Life Readings." From 1925 through 1944, he conducted some 2,500 of these Life Readings. Included in these were remarkable readings about soul life and how every soul had been alive and active since the Creator first said, "Let there be Light." When Cayce died on January 3, 1945, he left 14,256 documented stenographic records of the readings he had given for more than 6,000 different people over a period of forty-three years. I have modernized the language, sentence structure, and syntax of his discourses to better approximate the way we read and speak the language today. The Edgar Cayce material is copyrighted by the Edgar Cayce Foundation and may not be used without permission.

The reader can judge for him- or herself whether these two Akashic source is valuable to the fuller understanding of how and why reincarnation occurs and karma plays its role in our lives.

Of course I have had my own intuitive perceptions and deep meditative awarenesses and insights that have added to my understanding over these forty plus years of research and study. I have traveled to most of the ancient sacred sites on this planet and read the ancient texts on walls of temples as well as papyruses and parchments.

As was once said by another researcher, I no longer believe in reincarnation and karma, I know it to be true. I have become aware of my soul's life and how it impacts my little, short incarnate life today, as well as how my incarnation life is affecting the whole of my soul's growth and understanding.

Reincarnation & Karma

"The way is open to my soul ... it sees the Great God...."
                    −Egyptian Book of the Dead

Ben Franklin on Reincarnation and Karma

"I believe ... that the soul of man is immortal and will be treated with justice in another life, respecting its conduct in this."

"I look upon death to be as necessary to the constitution as sleep. We shall rise refreshed in the morning."

Franklin wrote this epitaph at age 22:
The Body of B. Franklin Printer,
Like the Cover of an Old Book,
Its Contents Torn Out
And Stripped of its Lettering and Gilding,
Lies Here Food for Worms,
But the Work shall not be Lost,
For it Will as He Believed
Appear Once More
In a New and more Elegant Edition
Revised and Corrected
By the Author

1. THE MYSTERIES OF LIFE

I suppose all of us have, at one time or another, reflected on what is the meaning of life. Why do we exist? What is the purpose for life? Why do we live a life with so many achievements, relationships, memories, and growing understanding only to die and be separated from it all; or worse yet, to simply cease to exist? Could there be any hidden, longterm benefit from living a good life, a meaningful life, and developing skills and wisdom?

And why does life appear to be so unfair? For example, why is one child born handicapped or into poverty, disease, oppression, and an early death, while another is born healthy and into comfort, opportunity, and a long life? We hear news of an innocent person being brutally victimized by a total stranger and wonder how there could be any sense to this. And why are some people starving while others struggle to eat less? One person takes a chance and makes a fortune, another loses everything. Why? How are these people chosen? What forces are involved in these situations, if any? Is it all the result of unpredictable forces of Nature, a great big game of chance? Or is there some understandable plan behind all that we see and experience?

Another of life's puzzles is why are each of us born with different talents? How can a six-year-old

Mozart write a symphony as well or better than people who have studied music all their lives? Where does this ability come from? Obviously, it doesn't have to be learned since you can be *born* with the talent. But why does one person have it and another not?

Life is a mystery. And something within drives us to find purpose and meaning in it. Very few of us live well without at least a sense of purpose and meaning. And yet, few of us claim to have seen the whole picture in the many pieces of puzzle of life.

Science and Religion

In the Western world there are two dominant sources providing information regarding these questions. They are science and religion. Both try to unravel the mysteries of life and provide answers to help explain the nature of and purpose for our lives. To a limited extent they even try to explain the causes behind the circumstances of our lives – why it is the way it is, why some of us succeed and some fail, why some suffer and others go merrily along.

For the most part, science has built its set of beliefs on *observable* phenomena, *substantiated* by tests. To a great extent, science, by its very nature, is centered around the observable universe, and for the most part it relies on the perceptive powers of the five senses and the enhancement of these with instruments. Beyond sensually observed phenomena, it classifies most everything as *theory*. Therefore, reality, according to science, is what has been observed to be so and can be substantiated through physical tests.

The driving force behind science is the pursuit of knowledge. Through investigation, study, hypotheses, and testing, knowledge is obtained. With knowledge will come understanding, and with enough knowledge the mystery can be solved.

Religion is quite different. Religious ideas have been built on centuries of human beliefs, feelings, thoughts and tenets and do not need to be observed by the senses or substantiated by tests. They are accepted as true because a significant number of the religion's adherents believe it to be so or because a great teacher has said it is so. In most cases the validity of the leader's teachings and the tenets of the followers are accepted as true because they are believed to have been Divinely inspired.

The driving force behind religion is not knowledge; in fact, knowledge is seen as one of the causes of "original sin." Adam and Eve ate from the "Tree of the Knowledge of Good and Evil," and that caused all their problems, and ours through their legacy. For religion, *faith* brings one through the mysteries to a peace with life's many mysteries. The faithful, it is said, will eventually know the truth, and that truth will set them free.

Where science seeks knowledge, religion seeks faithfulness to the tenets. Where science gains through investigation, religion gains through living the tenets, and in some cases through inspiration and even personal revelation. Where science uses reason and observation to identify truth, religion uses emotion and miraculous signs to indicate the presence of truth. Religion touches the heart, science touches the mind – oops, most scientists would say it touches only the observable *electro-chemical brain*. The mind is something beyond physical reality and lies in the realm of psychology, which is hardly a science.

Let's briefly look at the major concepts in these two dominant sources of Western understanding.

SCIENCE

Science predominantly defines life in biological terms. Something is "alive" if it manifests certain biological conditions, namely: growth through metabolism, the ability to adapt to its environment through changes originating internally, and the ability to reproduce itself. By this definition a rock is not alive and an amoeba is.

Added to the biological quality of being alive, science observes levels of "aliveness" – an amoeba may well be alive, but its level of awareness or consciousness in no way compares with that of a monkey. The monkey is more alive because it is not only biologically living through metabolism, reproduction, and adapting to changing conditions, but it is also *perceiving* more of its inner and outer environment. It displays the conditions of having attitudes, emotions, and memories, as well as the powers of thinking, learning, and communicating.

When science looks around the observable world it sees gradations of "aliveness" from the merely biological to the highly conscious forms of life, and it sees evidence that these gradations have evolved from the simple to the complex over long periods of time. At present, science finds enough evidence to propose that the origin of human life was a fortuitous event in the waters of this planet millions of years ago in which circumstances were just right for the emergence of biological life in its simplest form. Of course physics, a fundamental science, teaches that the ingredients for our life came from exploding stars whose elements landed on this watery planet. We are composed of stardust.

Physicist Lawrence Krauss: "Every atom in your body came from a star that exploded. And, the atoms in your left hand probably came from a different star than the atoms in your right hand. It really is the most poetic thing I know about the universe: You are all stardust. You couldn't be here if stars hadn't exploded, because the elements (the carbon, nitrogen, oxygen, all the things that matter for evolution) weren't created at the beginning of time. So forget Jesus. Stars died so you could live." (Lawrence M. Krauss, *A Universe from Nothing*, Atria Books, 2013, and AAI 2009)

Of course Dr. Krauss is talking about our physical bodies and Jesus was talking about our souls. Souls? Where are they? We'll get to them in an upcoming section.

Science's view of life, though contributing to the overall picture of the processes involved in life, does not give much meaning to an individual life. As of yet, science observes the apparent purpose for life to be the perfection of the species through "survival of the fittest." Since one's life is determined by *genetic* structure and *physical* environment, the circumstances in one's life are a result of the forces of Nature.

An individual seeking answers, reasons, and meaning finds that life can be scientifically described as little more than the result of the random contact of one single sperm cell (out of millions of sperm cells) with one egg, and the subsequent division of these cells, following a genetic code inside these cells. This group of cells, now forming a body, will live for about 70 to 100 years if it isn't destroyed by disease or some unfortunate incident, and will then stop living. It will cease to exist. Death is the end of life. Our species will go on perfecting the life-form through the genes passed on by the parents, but the parents' bodies are no more. New beings will rise up, live in their glory, pass on their genes, and then decay and die.

Perhaps sometime in the future science will discover a way for individuals to live much longer or even indefinitely, but for now, death is unavoidable. And even if science learns how to prolong life there is no evidence it will provide insight into its meaning.

RELIGION

Religion, specifically Western, Judeo-Christian religion, teaches that all life was created by a divine being. Though mysterious for man to understand, the creator's ways are purposeful and have meaningful, and this life is intentional, not random.

In such a religious belief structure, man is God's greatest creation. The individual human being is more than a biological organism; it is a "soul" or "spirit" which lives *beyond* the death of biological body. In this way, the life of an individual is not lost at death but goes on. All its achievements, joys, loves, and memories are not ended, but contribute to the individual's life after death. Accordingly, man has the opportunity to live forever with God in heaven after his or her earthly life ends.

Religion even provides explanations for suffering and misfortune, which can be outlined as follows.

1) Original Sin. This type of suffering is the result of a sin committed by man's ancestors, Adam and Eve. According to Western religion they were the first man and woman to be created and from whom all others have come. These two lived with God in the Garden of Eden and walked with Him daily. But they ate a forbidden fruit from "the tree of the knowledge of good and evil" and for this offense they were banished from the garden and the company of God. Consequently, life on earth is far from what it might have been.
2) The second reason for suffering and disappointment is misuse of one's "free will." Whenever one's will crosses the will of God, the individual experiences discomfort, suffering, and disappointment. the Old Testament is filled with such teachings and examples.

3) The third type of suffering comes not as a result of *previous* free-will actions, but because there is an inherent value in the process of suffering. One learns a lesson that could not be gained otherwise and grows wiser as a result. And these tests or lessons are supported by the Creator, as indicated in the Bible book of Job, where God enlists the help of Satan to test Job's faith and love for God. In Job's case, he passes the test and a hundredfold of what he lost during the test is restored to him.

Western religions hold that a person's biological life on Earth is an opportunity to live according to a code of moral and behavioral guidelines in such a way as to *earn* the privilege of entering heaven after death and living with God. Heaven is the home of the divine creator and is a joyous place to abide.

If one does not do well according to the moral and behavioral codes, he will enter one of two other places: purgatory or hell (this teaching varies with religious sects). In purgatory the soul suffers hard for its sins, but as the name implies, it is eventually *purged* of evil and freed to enter heaven. If, however, its sins are too grievous, the soul enters hell forever. Here it suffers excruciating pain without end.

Even though religion provides man with meaning and purpose, it leaves many important questions unanswered. Sometimes it seems to create more questions than it answers. Questions like: If this life is an opportunity to live in such a way as to earn the privilege to enter heaven, why then are we all not given the same opportunity to live this life well? Why are some souls born into environments of crime and sin, cruelty and violence, while others are born into constructive environments? Why are some of us born blind, crippled, or with a terrible disease? Why are some of us robbed, raped, or murdered? Why are some of us born into areas where the tenets of the religion aren't even known? And, why does God create a soul who had no choice in the matter of its coming into being only to eternally punish him severely because it didn't live up to the code required?

Despite these questions, religion contributes much to our lives and provides some key pieces to the puzzle of life, as does science.

THE HIDDEN TEACHINGS

There is another source for answers to the mysteries of life. And that is what this book is all about. This source is not as organized or well-defined as science and religion. But its explanations hold together so well and are so comprehensive that many people seriously study them and attempt to live by their perspective.

Unfortunately, this source has no unifying name to its body of knowledge. Various parts of its principal concepts are actually scattered throughout different cultures and texts with no central collection point for the ideas. Because of this, and because many of its ideas are not widely known (this is due in part to the adherents of these ideas purposefully withholding the teachings from the broader public), I'll refer to this school of thought as the Secret or Hidden Teachings. But it is not a single school of thought; rather, it's a hodgepodge of concepts from many diverse and often unrelated sources that possess similar views of life and its meaning. And many of these teachings come from ancient cultures of the Western world, such as ancient Egypt, but also elements of these teachings are found in the Eastern teachings of Hinduism, Buddhism, and Taoism.

Science would categorize the hidden teachings as *metaphysical*, meaning "beyond the known laws and observations of physics." Religion might refer to them as *mystical*, meaning that they belong to a collection of thought considered to be too mysterious to consider, or of dubious origin. And yet the Torah and Bible contain some of the most mysterious texts one can read! Even so, mysticism if not part the main lessons in Western religions.

Yet, it is interesting to note that the great religions have *sects* within them that know of and ascribe to some or all of the mystical teachings! Judaism has Kabbalah, early Christianity has Gnosticism and several renown mystics, and Islam once had Sufism (initially mystical but has recently become fundamentalistic).

Science, too, has had its adherents to concepts held by the secret teachings. Many scientists have written about theories of life *beyond* the physically observable. In some cases, phenomena has forced them to consider new theories. For example, medical science has found that patients who have been declared dead, then revived through the miracles of modern medicine, have reported witnessing the events occurring in the operating or emergency room while they were "dead"! Since their bodies were obviously dead on the table, it should have been impossible for them to witness anything that transpired from the time they "died" until the time the doctors revived them. Though their stories vary, generally the patients claim to have been outside of their bodies, observing the whole process from above the scene or from across the room. They claim to have looked back and seen their bodies on the table, dead. The doctors and nurses would then go into their special action plan for reviving a dead body using chemicals, electricity ("clear!"), and physical manipulations, such as pounding on the chest or massaging the heart. Later the doctor would come into the Recovery Room to see how his or her patient was doing, only to hear a story that was impossible to explain according to current theories of life. Apparently, some part of an individual remained alive while the body was definitely dead, and some portion of the dead person observed what was going on! The are some 30 books on Amazon describing what is now known as a "near-death experience." But the doctors assure us that there was nothing "near" about it – the patient was dead by all measurements: no heartbeat, no breathing, no life signs , no blood flowing to the brain. Their bodies had stopped functioning.

In another example we find researchers observing that learned traits may possibly be passed on to others without any means of physical contact. In his book *The Hundredth Monkey*, Ken Keyes Jr. reported the following:

The Japanese monkey, Macaca Fuscata, had been observed in the wild for a period of over 30 years. In 1952, on the island of Koshima, scientists were providing monkeys with sweet potatoes dropped in the sand. The monkeys liked the taste of the raw sweet potatoes but they found the sand unpleasant. An 18-month-old female named *Imo* found she could solve the problem by washing the potatoes in a nearby stream. She taught this trick to her mother. Her playmates also learned this new way and they taught their mothers too. This cultural innovation was gradually picked up by various monkeys before the eyes of the scientists. Between 1952 and 1958 all the young monkeys learned to wash the sandy sweet potatoes to make them more palatable. Only the adults who imitated their children learned this social improvement. Other adults kept eating the sandy sweet potatoes. Then something startling took place. In the autumn of 1958, a certain number of Koshima monkeys were washing sweet potatoes (the exact number is not known). Let us suppose that when the sun rose one morning there were 99 monkeys on Koshima Island who had learned to wash their sweet potatoes. Let's further suppose that later that morning, the hundredth monkey learned to wash potatoes. By that evening almost every monkey in the tribe was washing sweet potatoes before eating them. The added energy of this hundredth monkey somehow created an ideological breakthrough!

A most surprising thing observed by these scientists was that the habit of washing sweet potatoes then jumped over the sea! Colonies of monkeys on other islands and the mainland troop of monkeys at Takasakiyama began washing their sweet potatoes. Thus, when a certain critical number achieves an awareness, this new awareness may be communicated from mind to mind. Although the exact number may vary, this Hundredth Monkey Phenomenon means that when only a limited number of people know of a new way, it may remain the conscious property of those people. But there is a point at which if only one more person tunes in to a new awareness, a field is strengthened so that this awareness is picked up by almost everyone!

From such knowledge, some scientists are developing theories beyond physically observable phenomena, opening us up to a new vision of life – life beyond the physical – a life that may include a "collective consciousness" to which all humans are attuned.

Adding to the Hundredth Monkey concept are studies that show that all humans around the planet, without regard for their cultural or genetic circumstances, dream. But even more amazing is that they all have the *same* themes in their dreams, regardless of their environment or upbringing!

And one of American's great universities, the University of Virginia, has completed years of research into evidence of past-life memory among young people in cultures where such knowledge is not suppressed or seen as nonsense. Ian Stevenson, M.D., the late Psychiatrist at the University of Virginia School of Medicine, Chair of the Department of Psychiatry, and Director of the Division of Perceptual Studies, published these findings in his books *20 Cases Suggestive of Reincarnation*, *Children Who Remember Previous Lives*, and *Where Reincarnation and Biology Intersect*. Subsequent to Dr. Stevenson's findings Edward F. Kelly, Adam Crabtree, and Paul Marshall edited a cutting-edge book detailing the mounting evidence of life beyond physicality in their book *Beyond Physicalism: Toward Reconciliation of Science and Spirituality* (Rowman & Littlefield, 2015).

The hidden teachings possess many wonderful insights into the whys and hows of life, giving us a much broader picture of our nature and our life.

In the following chapters the secret teachings will be described in as much detail as I can gather together from the many and varied sources. In addition to mystical religious and metaphysical scientific sources, I have found elements of the hidden teachings in obscure legends and myths, teachings of minor prophets and philosophers, and in the ancient records recovered by archeologists. Much of my initial understanding of these teachings came from the work of the relatively modern (1877-1945) mystic and psychic, Edgar Cayce, who could read the Hinduism called the *Akasha* – referring to the essence of life and the records of its activity since, during, and following the creation. It is a record that is recorded in the "ethers," not in stone or on parchment. It has been referred to as "The Book of Life" or "The Book of Remembrance." It may also be thought of as a collective mind upon which all the activities and thoughts of every individual mind make an impression, an impression that can be known or "read," as Edgar Cayce revealed over some forty years. Of course, it is for you to determine the value of this information.

Perhaps you'll find, as I have, that the secret teachings possess an unusually comprehensive view of life and answer many of the questions we've all considered to be unanswerable.

In order to understand life as it is seen in the hidden teachings we must go back to the story of the original creation and retell it, for today's version is not quite correct.

The following is the story of Creation – with all of its purposes and influence in our lives today – according to the secret teachings.

Leo Tolstoy on Reincarnation

"As we live through thousands of dreams in our present life, so is our present life only one of many thousands of such lives which we enter from the other, more real life and then return after death. Our life is but one of the dreams of that more real life, and so it is endlessly, until the very last one, the very real, the life of God."

2. OVERLOOKED MESSAGES IN GENESIS

According to the secret teachings, the universe was not first created in matter but existed prior to the material creation. Consider how the Bible book of Genesis tells of two creations, the first in chapter one when we were conceived in the image of God (Genesis 1:26) and then another creation in chapter two using the "dust of the ground" and the "breath of life" (Genesis 2:7). Technically speaking there was a *third* creation! It is recorded later in chapter 2 verse 21-25, the Creator caused a deep sleep to fall over the initially androgynous, hermaphroditic being, and subsequently separates the feminine and the masculine into gender-specific bodies. The initial oneness of ancient Yin and Yang was not separated.

Many of the teachings of ancient cultures contains legends of *two* creations. The first creation ultimately failed, forcing a second creation. And it is this second creation that you and I are most familiar with. But let's begin with the First Creation.

Imagine the universe *before* the beginning, before anything existed – nothing, absolutely nothing – emptiness for as far as you could see and hear in any direction. Yet the force that would begin the creation *was there*. Within this pre-creation void there existed the "first impulse," the "first cause," the initial motivative influence that would bring forth the creation. In this emptiness existed that which was *before* the so-called "Big Bang."

One way for us to conceive of how there could be absolute emptiness and yet something in this emptiness to cause the beginning is to imagine a *consciousness* similar to our own, except that this first consciousness was a boundless, universal consciousness with no thoughts in it – perfectly still. But like a consciousness, it was alive and possessed the potential conceive within the womb of its mind. Using this image, if we looked through the pre-creation emptiness for the Creator, the "first impulse," we would actually be standing within the universe's infinite, quiet consciousness. The creation would begin much like a clear mind begins to conceive.

At some moment, this First Consciousness desired to express Itself. Stirring from Its silence, It began to conceive, to imagine and express Its inner promptings. And so the creation began – light, sound ... eventually stars, galaxies, trees, and rivers.

This point in creation is still *prior* to the physical creation that science records. This is a realm of *thought*, no physical forms exist, only thoughts in the consciousness of the Universe. Genesis records it this way:

These are the generations of the heavens and of the earth when they were created, in the day that the Lord God made the earth and the heavens, and every plant of the field *before* it was in the earth, and every herb of the field *before* it grew; for the Lord God had not caused it to rain upon the earth, and there was *not* a man to till the ground. (Genesis 2:4-5, my italics)

Now keep in mind that in the first chapter of Genesis God had created everything, including man in His/Her image. Chapter two even opens with this line:

"Thus the heavens and the earth were finished, and all the host of them." (Genesis 2:1) But this was in consciousness not in matter or materiality.

This is difficult to comprehend, but perhaps if you close your eyes and imagine that you are a mind, that is temporarily incarnating in a physical organism for about 80 to 100 years.

So to clarify, the *idea* of light was conceived, the *idea* of a river, but not the *physical form*. The physical, three-dimensional universe had not yet been created. It was all in higher dimensions of life. This is a fundamental belief in most ancient lore around this planet. Of course I realize that our evolutionary view of life causes us to discredit ancient cultures as immature, and that we are the apex of evolution. But there are megalithic structures around this planet that are so perfectly carved and oriented to stellar cycles and magnetic fields, that some of the ancients were not just cavemen or corn growers.

According to the secret teachings, there came a point in this initial creation where the Creator's Consciousness conceived angels, souls, and humanity. Within the One Universal Consciousness many individual points of consciousness were given existence.

Edgar Cayce, the amazing psychic reader of the Akashic Records or the Book of Life, gave the following:

Individuals in the beginning were more of thought forms than individual entities with personalities as seen in the present ... and their projections into the realms of fields of thought that pertain to a developing or evolving world of matter.... Hence we find occult or psychic science, as would be called at the present, was rather the natural state of man in the beginning. (EC 364-10)

It's important for us to realize that at this point in our existence we did not have physical bodies. All of what I've just described occurred within the Mind of God. Consequently, its "form" resembled that of thought rather than three-dimensional objects composed of matter. In the very beginning we were individual points of consciousness within the one great Universal Consciousness. And this is not a farfetched idea, even scientists agree that only four percent of the universe is visible matter! Ninety-six percent of the universe is invisible to us. However, its presence can be determined by its effect on the visible.

At first our bodiless essence was still, our wills content to observe the wonders of the creation as they flowed from the Mind of God. In these early periods we were so much a part of the Creator's Consciousness that we were one with It, and virtually indistinguishable from It. At first, we simply imitated the Creator. But eventually we began to use our wills to express ourselves or to react to expressions. We began to develop individual memories and motivations, causing us have a slightly different complex of being other beings. This individuation began what we call today our "soul." Our souls gained experience, and with experience came knowledge and confidence. Then, we truly began to create on our own, adding new dimensions to the creation, much like a second voice adds to a song by singing harmony with the main melody.

And according to many ancient legends this was exactly why we had been created – to share in and contribute to the great expression of Life. Harmony and oneness with our Creator was the ideal. We were to be cooperative companions of the Creator and all of the creation. To fulfill this purpose we were created in the image of the Creator: consciousness with freedom, capable of conceiving, perceiving, and remembering; capable of communicating directly with the Creator and the creation.

Edgar Cayce's reading of the Book of Life gave this perspective and motivation for our souls: "As the entity moves from sphere to sphere, it seeks its way to the home, to the face of the Creator, the Father, the first cause." (EC 136-8) Cayce identified the first cause as: "That the created would be the companion for the Creator." This is the reason we were created, and as a result, the created (our soul) is given opportunities to "show itself to be not only worthy of, but companionable to, the Creator." (EC 5753-1) Since we are talking about the Creator of the entire Cosmos and everything in it, we are celestial star travelers, even though we feel so earthly and terrestrial in our daily physical lives.

Our initial being and oneness was as a soul group and is recorded in the Bible book of Job, 38:7: "The morning stars sang together and all the children of God shouted for joy (at the coming of humanity)." Our souls were the among the morning stars, and were a soul group moving harmoniously like a flock of birds, a school of fish. Of course were a harmonious flock of interconnected *minds* and *souls*.

Edgar Cayce gave these readings for the beginning of two people who came to him for insight about their souls:

We find in the beginning, when the first of the elements were given, and the forces set in motion that brought about the sphere as we find called earth plane, and when the morning stars sang together, and the whispering winds brought the news of the coming of man's indwelling.... This entity came into being with this multitude. (EC 294-8)

We find the entity was among those in the day when the forces of the Universe came together, when there was upon the waters the sound of the coming together of the Sons of God, when the morning stars sang together, and over the face of the waters there was the voice of the glory of the coming of the plane for man's dwelling. In all of these we find some of this present entity's individuality ... are brought through. (EC 341-1)

Consciousness and free will were the greatest qualities given any creation, but they came with equally great responsibility for their use or misuse. Of course, the all-knowing Universal Mind knew the potential dangers in giving beings complete freedom to do as they desired. It did so for the potential joy of sharing life with true companions, not servants or automatons. Therefore, each of these new free-willed beings would simply have to learn to master the urges and to subdue harmful desires in order to live in harmony with the other creatures and the Creator. To do otherwise would only bring disharmony, suffering, and aloneness.

Cayce's readings give this insight: "The intention was to be able to partake of the physical but not be a part of same. More and more [you need to be] feeding upon those sources from which you emanate, or of the SPIRITUAL life, so that the physical body, the mental body are attuned to your soul forces, your soul source, your Creator, your Maker, in such a way and manner as you develop. (EC 364-10)

The legends tell that chaos came. As we continued to use our godly powers we became more fascinated with them. We began to focus more and more on our own creations and became less concerned with and attentive to their harmony with the Creator, with the Whole. The more we thought of just ourselves and our own desires with less regard for the Whole, the more self-centered we became, eventually perceiving ourselves as separate from the Whole.

Of course, this sense of separation was all in our heads, so to speak, because there really was no way we could exist outside of the Whole. It was more a result of our sustained focus of attention on ourselves and our self-interests that resulted in a narrower awareness centered around self.

This was the beginning of trouble. It led to a very long fall for us. A fall that eventually left us feeling alone and separated from the rest of life, even to the point that we, who were actually companions and co-creators with the Universal Creator, came to think of ourselves as little more than dust-like creatures, descendants of apes, and inhabitants of a planet on the outskirts of a very typical galaxy in the endless and diverse universe.

To know ourselves to be ourselves and yet one with the Whole was the ideal condition, but the centering of awareness on self alone resulted in a sense of separation from the Whole. The more we exercised our individual consciousness and free will for self-interest, self-gratification, self-glorification and self-consciousness, the more we heightened our sense of self apart from the Whole.

The resulting loss of contact with the Source of our life and the purpose for our existence was the beginning of darkness and evil. Without a clear sense of our relationship to the rest of life, many of us began to use free will in ways that were never meant to be. Others simply let themselves be carried along with the current of life, abdicating their free will to the will of others. In both cases, our naive curiosity, combined with a reckless disregard for the consequences of our actions and thoughts, and our relentless self-seeking caused us to do and experience many things that we would come to regret – things that would make it very difficult for us to be companions to the Creator.

However, the Creator foresaw this potential and, prior to creating companions, It created a Universal Law: Whatever one did with its free will, it must experience. The law was not intended as punishment or retribution for offenses, but as a tool for education and enlightenment. Thus, as we used our freedom we experienced the effects. In this way we came to understand and learn.

Interestingly, science and religion recognize this law. In science it is often stated, "For every action there is a reaction." Its religious counterpart is, "An eye for an eye, a tooth for a tooth;" "As you sow, so shall you reap;" and "As you do unto others, it will be done unto you." Even the kids on our streets know something of this law, expressing its principle in their saying, "What goes around, comes around."

This is the law of Karma, of cause and effect. It is the great teacher of the companions-to-be and it is an integral part of the secret teachings. However, as we will see in a later chapter, the secret teachings develop an entire vision of life around the tireless, precise workings of this fundamental law of the universe.

Once this law was established, the Creator conceived and freed countless independent points of consciousness within Its own infinite consciousness and the companions came into being, each conscious and free. What a trembling wonder it must have been in those first moments.

Again, it's important to realize that the companions were not physical bodies. They were like "ideas" in the mind of the Creator that were given freedom to be independently conscious. As they used their freedom they developed into unique points of thought, feeling, desire, expression and memory. Each was slightly different from the other by virtue of their different vantage point within the Universal Consciousness and by the different ways they acted and reacted to life around and within themselves. They were developing ideas, becoming clearer and more uniquely defined and identifiable as they experienced life; but like an idea, they were not three-dimensional form. Their true "form" was consciousness.

Let me try to describe the companions' nature using terms we are familiar with today. Each has spirit, mind and soul. Spirit is the essence of life. Remember the condition of the Creator before the creation; alive yet still. Nothing existed, but life was latent in the emptiness like a consciousness without a thought. This is Spirit, as I'm defining it here. It is the living stillness in the midst of activity. So often we identify life with motion, but the essence of life was there before the motion. Spirit is the essence of life.

Life in motion, or the power to move and shape ideas and even physical forms out of spirit, is mind. Mind is the sculptor, the builder who conceives, imagines and shapes ideas out of the essence of life. Spirit is life; Mind is the power to use it.

Using these definitions, a rock would be considered alive. Spirit's presence in the rock is certainly different from that of the amoeba, but a rock has spirit. Mind has shaped this aspect of life into a hard, seemingly motionless form, but, as the Native Americans and most indigenous peoples always knew, rock has spirit. Just wear a crystal or a lapis for a month and see if you aren't influenced by the vibrations coming off of these "rocks."

Each of the companions had spirit and mind. As they used their life forces they developed experiences, memories, desires, fears, etc. This caused them to become unique from one another – each having its own collection of experiences and aspirations; each its own story. This individual aspect of the companion is its soul. Soul is the sum total of all the companion has done with its free-willed consciousness. It's the companion's story, its complex of memories. All of the companions have Spirit and Mind but each developed a unique Soul, because each built a different collection of memories and experiences, resulting in different desires, hopes and attitudes about life.

As you can see, the soul developed, grew and changed, just as it continues to do in the present. It changes as the individual lives and experiences life and gradually builds its own collection of memories which result in a unique character.

Spirit is the life force, Mind is the power to use it and Soul is the being that develops. All are one in consciousness.

INTO THE EARTH

The creation progressed from essence to thought, thought into thought-form, and from thought-form into particle-form or atomic-form; in other words, matter. There are many dimensions to life. One of them is the third dimension – physical form as we know it today.

The companions, filled with their new-found consciousness and freedom, went out into the vast universe to experience life and to learn about themselves, the Creator, and their relationship to It. In their travels through the cosmos, some of the companions entered the three-dimensional influences of the planet Earth where they entered into physical form for the first time. Here they became so encapsulated in the physical that they began to identify themselves more with their form than with their consciousness. They began to think of themselves as physical entities rather than free, living consciousnesses. Incredibly, these celestial beings began to think they were only terrestrial beings. Form was so substantial, so captivating, that it was difficult to hold onto the more delicate reality of spirit-thoughts, pure points of consciousness in a Universal Consciousness.

To have an individual body was also the ultimate in self-identity, self-expression. It had the power of separating one from the Whole and the formless spirit-thoughts of higher dimensions.

Strong identification with the physical made the companions subject to the laws of Nature, and, of course, a part of Nature's cycle was death. The body would come to life according to the laws of Nature, live for a time and then die. In their original state, the companions were continually alive, but those that began to strongly identify with their physical bodies were now affected by death. Since they thought they were their bodies, they considered themselves dead when their bodies died. And for all intents and purposes they were dead. "As the mind thinks, so it is."

This was a serious confusion, and when the companions who had not become involved with the Earth saw what had happened to the others, they decided to help those on Earth regain their former state. However, it was not going to be easy. The Earthbound companions had continued in this masquerade for so long they were deeply possessed by the belief that the physical world was the real world, even to the point that all else seemed like phantoms and dreams. Life for them had become totally physical.

They considered themselves lucky to live a long physical life, expecting to eventually die like all those that had come before them. That's as far as their limited vision could take them.

In addition to the influences of the physical dimension, the souls were building reaction patterns (karmic patterns) with their willful activities in the physical world. According to the universal law, these actions had to be met – properly met in the physical where they had been initiated. So the web was becoming more and more entangled and complex. The more one acted in the Earth environs, the more one built Earth-debts that had to be met in future Earth-reactions. There were going to be no quick outs for anyone. Once a soul touched the physical, it was certain to become possessed and confused by the very nature of the realm. The only joys found in the physical would be those of the Spirit and these would be so delicate or intangible that it would be difficult to hold onto them – not impossible, but difficult.

Of course, the pleasures of the physical would be fulfilling to the physical aspect of these incarnated souls, but it would not sustain them for very long. They were children of the cosmos, celestial beings; terrestrial pleasures could only hold their interests so long before they desired experiences more true to their real nature. Yet, by the very nature of the flesh, it would be hard to free the spirit from it.

Another effect of entering the Earth plane was the division of consciousness. According to the concepts found in the Edgar Cayce revelations (see Appendix for background on Edgar Cayce), as an individual entered deeper into the physical, its consciousness separated into three divisions of awareness. Two of these divisions we acknowledge today, the conscious and subconscious. The first entails the physical world where the human body required a three-dimensional consciousness to function in the Earth. It has become the part of our consciousness we are most familiar with, what we have come to call the conscious mind. Many of us would consider it to actually be the "I" or "me" of ourselves. It is within this part of consciousness that we experience physical life, and our personalities are developed. In many ways it is our Earth-self.

The second part of consciousness is shadow-like while one is incarnate. It lives life like a shadow, always there, listening, watching, remembering and only occasionally making its profound and sometimes frightening presence known. We have come to call this part of our consciousness the subconscious mind. From out of this area come dreams, intuitions, unseen motivations, and deepest memories. According to many teachings, the subconscious is the realm of the soul which uses the conscious mind as a mechanism for manifesting in the physical plane through the five senses. Often the thoughts and interests of the conscious mind, combined with the desires of the body, become so strong and dominant that only its activities seem important and real; the subconscious seems illusionary and unrelated to outer life. But in truth, the real life is occurring in the subconscious. We'll explore this later on.

The third area of the now divided consciousness is the most universal. It is the part that can perceive and commune with the Universal Consciousness. We have different names for it: the Collective Mind, the Universal Mind, the Collective Unconscious, and Cayce's term, the Superconscious.

As seen in the following diagram, the more one's attention moves into the conscious mind, the more narrow and limited the focus and awareness become.

The more one moves toward the superconscious, the more one expands awareness and becomes aware of the Whole, the Universal Forces, the Creator.

Levels of Consciousness

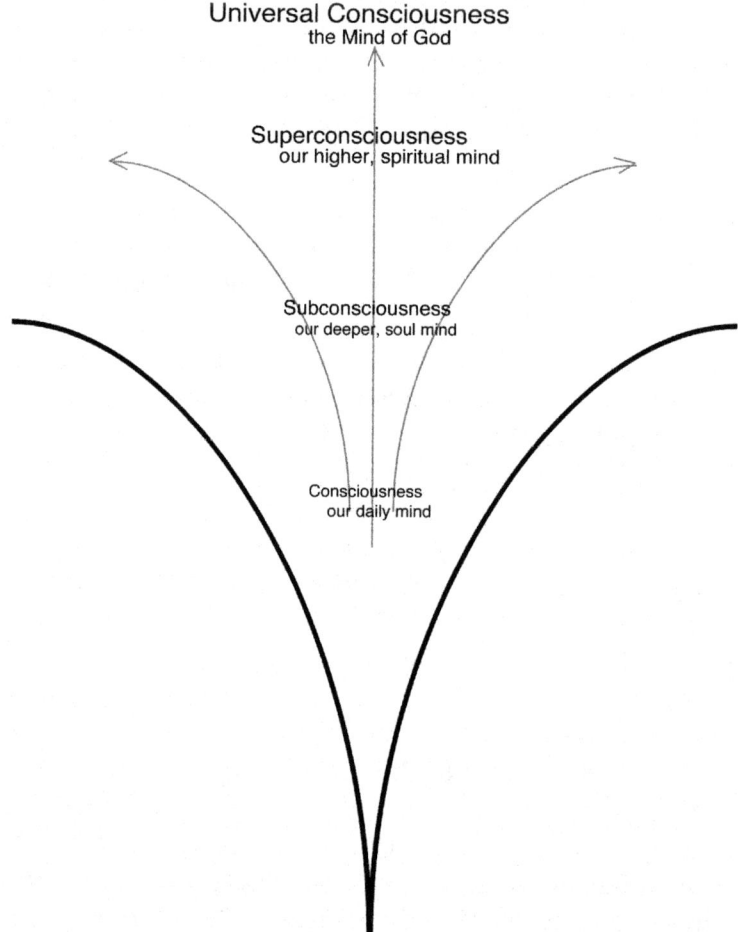

It may be more difficult to perceive the infinite when one is grossly involved in the finite, but the Universal Consciousness and the potential for attuning oneself to It remains. Curiously, the access is through the inner consciousnesses of the incarnate individual and not outside of it, making it a very mysterious passage for a physical being.

In time, however, the Earthbound companions could again become aware of the difference between terrestrial life and celestial. They could again come to know their original state and purpose, and regain their celestial birthright of companionship with the Creator. In time they could again come to realize that the conditions in their present physical life were the result of their free-will actions and choices before the present life.

They could even come again to know themselves as co-creators with their Creator. The Creator is considered to be both genders in oneness (yin and yang united), complete unto Itself, but our language does not allow for a pronoun to express this nature, so I'll occasionally use the capitalized "He/She" or "Him/Her" to keep from masculinizing the Creator. I'll also use the neutral pronoun, "It," to keep from personifying the Universal Consciousness too much. It is personal, but not a person as we know them.

If the Earthbound souls could genuinely begin to believe that the physical cannot possibly be all there is to life, they could begin the long journey back from form to spirit, a very difficult journey. One simply cannot think of oneself as a lump of flesh, blood and bone one minute and as ethereal, spirit-form in the next minute. The influences of finite form on an infinite being are profoundly stupefying. In many ways we, as human beings, are no longer spirit. Flesh has become very much a part of us, not just physically but mentally, as well. Even when we are out of the body (through death, deep sleep or some altered state), bodily manifestation is still very much a part of us.

Otherwise, there would certainly be no reincarnation. We would simply leave and never return.

Furthermore, Christ's incarnation would mean much less than it does. There would be no significance to the resurrection of the body if the body were of no value or purpose. As it is, flesh is now a part of our total being. It is worthy of resurrection and salvation, rather than destruction and abandonment.

The great paradox of man is that he is now both spirit and flesh. That's like saying we are a combination of oil and water, two substances which do not combine. I suppose the mystical analogy would more properly be fire and water; these too don't combine. How can anything be made up of two substances that are impossible to combine? Yet, such is the nature of humanity. We are constantly forced to reconcile the seemingly unreconcilable: mercy with justice, cooperation with independence, unity with diversity, tradition with change, feeling with thought, love with truth, and on and on. In the Cayce material the warning to seekers of enlightenment is often, seek a balance! Perhaps this is also the intention behind Jesus' teaching that, "in patience possess ye your soul." Patience is certainly required if one is to reconcile spirit with flesh.

3. A STELLAR DIMENSION

Entering the influences of the Earth was not a quick, single transition from spirit to form, from universal consciousness to physical consciousness, but a long descent through many levels of consciousness and realms of activity. It also didn't begin with the Earth. Souls experienced many parts of the Universe, including other planets. Many still do. Even more fascinating is the concept that a soul is not bound to the physical world even when incarnate! Depending on its level of awareness, a soul may experience other dimensions while still incarnate.

According to the secret teachings, and particularly the Edgar Cayce material, Earth is not the only planet that attracts souls. As strange as it may sound given our current scientific beliefs, souls descending from out of the great Cosmos actually entered into this entire solar system, not just the Earth. They have had and continue to have experiences with other planets in this system, and some of the moons, and even the sun! Now, let me explain this before all my credibility vanishes.

The souls, being non-physical, were and are capable of sojourning in realms of consciousness beyond physical. This doesn't mean they live on the surface of other planets as we do on Earth, but rather in fourth and fifth dimensional realms associated with the planetary spheres that we see with our three-dimensional eyes. The physical planets are also non-physical realms which souls can experience when not actively in the physical body on Earth. This would include death, deep sleep, or other altered states that free the subconscious from its normal physical constraints.

Furthermore, each of the planets is a unique environ with activities that differ from other planets in this system. These activities can effect various changes in souls that experience them. It's as though the Solar System were a University in which the planets were various colleges within the university – a great big schoolhouse for the souls.

If a soul incarnates into an Earth-life from one of these planetary influences, it will manifest the influence of the realm from which it recently came. This is why astrology has so interested man since early history. The stars and planets have influence in peoples lives. Unfortunately, most of our modern astrologers have lost the original knowledge of why these spheres have influence. It is, according to the secret teachings, because reincarnating souls have not been in limbo prior to their return to Earth, but have actually been "traveling" among the stars and planets. (Remember, I am not talking about the physical stars and planets, but dimensions associated with the physical objects we see.) At the moment of birth, the position of the heavens gives some idea as to where the incarnating soul has been, and this in turn gives some idea of how he or she will behave in the current incarnation.

Let's look at each of these planets and their unique characteristics. They follow quite closely with astrology's knowledge of their influence. What follows are Edgar Cayce's descriptions of each planet's major influence on a soul:

Mercury pertains to the Mind and the mental abilities.

Venus pertains to Love, beauty and the arts.

Earth to the Flesh and the ability to actually prove one's inner beliefs through outer actions.

Mars pertains to "Madness" (Cayce's word), or the power of force, temper and drive – unless tempered by the mental forces.

Jupiter pertains to Strength, universality, expansiveness – dealing with groups or masses rather than individuals.

Saturn pertains always to Change – usually sudden or violent change; a preference to erase all and start over again. It is where flesh goes to purge itself (more on this in the chapter on Leila).

Uranus pertains to the Psychic abilities and occult sciences – and to extremes, such as: great goodness or badness, great wealth or poverty, etc.

Neptune pertains to the Mystic abilities, spiritual insight and a sense of the unseen – also some extremes unless tempered.

Pluto (possibly the same as Septimus and Vulcan) pertains to Consciousness, usually spiritual consciousness. Cayce said the influence of this planet is just beginning to enter Earth's environs.

The Cayce material indicates that an individual incarnating from the far-away planets of Uranus, Neptune and Pluto will seem peculiar, and will have difficulty being understood; while those incarnating from the nearby planets will seem more natural. Those from Venus will be inclined toward interests of love, caring, beauty and the arts; while those incarnating from Mercury will be inclined to mental powers and a mental approach to life – intellect, logic and mental gymnastics as opposed to the Venusians' feelings, emotions and cares of the heart. A soul who incarnates directly from a sojourn in the influences of Mars will possess urges to seek his or her way with force and power, influenced by temper and drive (unless such urges have been subdued; in this case, the soul may become a dynamic "doer" who also has patience.) General Patten, a believer in reincarnation, felt he was a son of Mars, a natural warrior. When we consider the "stellar dimension," he was probably correct. We could assume, following this concept, that his soul incarnated directly from a sojourn in the realms of Mars, bringing with it all the qualities that Mars would bestow on a soul.

Of course, many of us have experienced several planets from which we reflect multiple influences. Often Cayce would identify three or four planets as contributing to a person's total makeup. The "aspects" of planets one to another help to reveal a more complete picture of an individual's planetary influences. Multiple experiences also help to build a more balanced, multidimensional soul.

Judging from Patten's strengths, Mars would certainly have been a dominant force in his soul's experiences. But his weaknesses reveal limitations in the areas of diplomacy, compromise and patience. Perhaps, a few sojourns in Jupiter would have added helpful aspects to his character. And, according to the Cayce readings, this is exactly what may have occurred after his death. His soul, reflecting on the recent incarnation, may have decided that some new experiences were in order, and began a sojourn in the fourth dimensional realms of some "college" other than Mars.

Let's look at another example from the Cayce material, Cayce himself. According to the Cayce readings, the soul that came to be known as Edgar Cayce sojourned in the realms of Uranus prior to its incarnation as Edgar Cayce. On its way to Earth it briefly sojourned in the environs of Venus. Together these influences were in part responsible for Cayce's innate tendencies toward things of the psychic and an appreciation of beauty and art, and the power of love.

Planetary influences of the type I've described here, as opposed to astrology as it is practiced today, manifest themselves almost immediately in a child's preferences and approach to life. When the karmic influences (from previous Earth sojourns, not planetary sojourns) begin to manifest themselves (this usually occurs at or near puberty), then the combination of the planetary influences and the karmic influences, makes for the rocky teenage years.

Socrates on Reincarnation

"I am confident that there truly is such a thing as living again, that the living spring from the dead, and that the souls of the dead are in existence."

4. THE PHYSICAL BODY

When the companions began to enter, only the plant, animal and mineral kingdoms were on the Earth. Many of the first to arrive possessed whatever physical forms were available (companions had complete dominion over them) and just pushed their way into three-dimensional life. The bizarre creatures that remain in our legends today were the result of this forceful entry into early Earth: satyrs (beings that were half goat and half man), centaurs (half horse and half man), dryads (women living in trees, and often an entire "enchanted" forest of them), sphinxes (half man and half lion, ram or hawk; also a winged lion with a woman's head and breasts), and the mermaids.

Souls that did not immediately force their way in could see that assuming possession of these lower forms was not good; they desired to perfect a form especially for the companions. In this way the companions could manifest in a body more reflective of their true nature and not defy the law of nature which stated that all creatures should give life only to their own kind.

The rescuing souls began influencing the evolutionary cycles of the Earth forms until they could breed a form that closely approximated their ideal. The form they chose was indeed that of the apes, as our scientists have so carefully observed. Hovering over these ape creatures like Olympian gods, the companions used their creative powers to alter the monkey forms – something like a breeder would do to create a new species, but with much more power and influence.

The next step required the help of the Creator. In order for the form to be perfect for the companions, it needed to be enlivened by the original Creator of life. The companions, truly co-creators with God, had the power to create; having created many things, some beautiful, some ugly. But the final form for manifesting in the Earth needed that special spark of life that only the Creator could give. The Creator knew the needs of Its lost companions and their hearts, and lovingly added the final touch to the new physical form on the Earth, the human body. Perhaps this is why there remains a "missing link" in the evolutionary chain from ape to full man – the creative leap from ape to man being physically untraceable.

Once the human body was perfected, all those with strange, mixed-up bodies were corrected, until the companions were inhabiting only human bodies. No longer would human souls incarnate in animal, plant or mineral forms. The linger concept of transmigration is a carryover from this early period, but it doesn't occur today. In fact, the level of power possessed by most incarnating souls today is barely sufficient for them to completely possess human bodies.

The perfected bodies were then separated into two sexual forms, a male and a female. The companions had been androgynous in their spirit "form," male and female in one, but in order for them to manifest in the realm of duality it was necessary to divide these two aspects of soul.

Therefore, only one sexual aspect of an incarnate soul became dominantly manifested; usually it reflected the sex of the physical body, but not always. A soul could be manifesting its female aspect and yet incarnate in a male body. In such a case, we would see an effeminate male; in the reverse, we would see a masculine female. Usually, however, the male sexual aspect of the soul is expressed through a male body during incarnation, and the female aspect in a female body.

There were many reasons for separating these two sexual aspects of the soul while incarnating, the chief one being, of all things, loneliness. Togetherness in the celestial realm was natural, but the third dimension required clear demarcations of space and time. The souls were alone inside spatially separated bodies, and not only was it more difficult to companion with fellow souls, but because of the loss of contact with the Creator, one felt totally on one's own, without connection to anything but oneself. Therefore it was deemed best to separate the female and male aspects and create a relationship where two souls could reunite on the Earth and give some sense of wholeness and togetherness to Earthly life. It also provided a physically natural way to reproduce themselves according to the laws of nature. This would become very important as the companions continued to lose more and more cognizance of their spiritual selves, eventually becoming totally physical – completely subject to the laws of nature and without any supernatural power.

In the first chapters of Genesis we find a very similar description of the early periods in the Earth. Let me retell key parts of the Biblical Genesis and add the interpretations from the secret teachings.

Genesis 1:26 "And God said, 'Let us make man in our image, after our likeness: and let them have dominion over the fish of the sea, and over the fowl of the air, and over the cattle, and over all the Earth, and over every creeping thing that creeps upon the Earth.'"

Interpretation: God's companions are created in God's image, and like God, they are given power to do as they please with all of creation.

Genesis 1:27 "So God created man in his own image, in the image of God created he him; male and female created he them."

Interpretation: Each man is like God, having both the female and male aspects within himself. This is the spiritual creation of "man" or the souls. At this point they are only spiritual. The Earth is still without form but the idea of the Earth and its creatures has been created. Later in Genesis we find this:

Genesis 2:4-6 "These are the generations of the heavens and the Earth when they were created, in the day that the Lord God made the Earth and heavens, And every plant of the field before it was in the Earth, and every herb of the field before it grew: for the Lord God had not caused it to rain upon the Earth, and there was not a man to till the ground."

Interpretation: All of this is written after the seven days of creation had ended. Two creations were being described; the first occurred in the spirit, the second in the physical.

It is only after God created man in His image (1:27) that the Lord God creates a physical form for man to enter and live in while on the Earth, physically.

Genesis 2:7 "And the Lord God formed man of the dust of the ground, and breathed into his nostrils the breath of life; and man became a living soul."

Interpretation: According to the secret teachings, this is the creation of the body for manifesting in the

Earth. But it was the will of the soul that caused this to be done, not God's will, therefore the new name for this Creator, "Lord God," signifying a change. God had already finished the "seven days" of creation. Yet since the souls had forced themselves into the physical, it was necessary for them to have bodies of their own. However, even after this new body was completed, the souls were still not thriving. The nature of physical life was such that they were lonely.

Genesis 2:18, 22 "And the Lord God said, 'It is not good that the man be alone; I will make him an help meet for him.'...And from the rib, which the Lord God had taken from man, made he woman, and brought her unto the man."

Interpretation: From out of the initially androgynous being, the Lord God separated the female aspect and gave it a separate form. The ancient word for "rib" could also be interpreted as "side," indicating the female side of this male-female being. This left Adam changed; he was now male only and found companionship in his female half.

(Companionship is an innate urge of ours. Because God's motivation for creating us was companionship, we naturally feel a deep longing for it.)

The body that was eventually developed for the companions is like our body today. It possesses physical, mental and spiritual aspects. These parts are so closely blended together that the impressions of one have an effect on the other two: what one eats can affect one's thinking; thinking can affect digestion; spiritual inspiration can affect physical conditions; and so on. This is the vehicle of God's companions while they abide in the material plane and, as such, it has become the temple of the "living God."

According to nearly all the secret teachings, within this body are seven Spiritual Centers through which the soul manifests in the three-dimensional world. These centers (or chakras, as they are known in Eastern teachings) are associated with the endocrine glands and certain plexuses along the cerebrospinal and sympathetic nervous systems. Through these channels the forces of the spiritual reach into three-dimensional form providing the means for the incarnate soul to re-attune to its spiritual self and the Universal Consciousness.

These seven centers correlate with the seven colors of the spectrum that appear when a beam of white light is refracted. The symbology is subtly beautiful: the central, whole being is like a beam of white light; and as it passes through physical dimensions, represented by the prism (symbolizing the body), only its parts are seen.

The centers also correlate with the seven notes of the musical scale, and to seven major planets in our solar system, as indicated in the diagram and chart. The four lower centers correlate with the four elements of the Earth plane: earth, wind, water and fire. The four lower centers symbolize the Earth, while the three higher centers reflect Heaven.

The body of the companions is a reflection of their cosmic, universal selves, and as such, it is a temporary, terrestrial home for celestial beings.

ORIGINAL SIN

Before we get too far away from our new interpretation of the biblical Genesis, let's look at how man and woman originally sinned. From the secret teachings, we know that they were actually celestial beings who became terrestrial by their own doing, and eventually thought of themselves as little more than bodies. Furthermore, being in the physical plane was not their ultimate purpose for existence. It was hoped they would come to know and love God enough to seek

His/Her companionship in the spirit, not in the flesh (John 4:23-24). With all of this in mind, let's review the Genesis story of original sin.

The Earthbound souls, now represented by Adam and Eve, were forbidden to eat the fruit from the "Tree of the Knowledge of Good and Evil" because if they did, as the serpent well knew (Gen. 3:4-5), they would know they were really gods within God and had free will to do whatever they pleased. (The serpent neglected to tell them that they had already used their free will to force their way into the Earth, an act they would not be proud of if they knew the difference between good and evil – especially if they became aware of it before they were ready to face God with such knowledge.) And, if they ate the fruit before they were ready, their shame and guilt would so overwhelm them that they would not want to be near God's all-knowing consciousness. Thus, restricting their awareness of good and evil gave them time to live in God's manifested presence (represented by the new names, Lord God and Lord) and gradually regain an awareness of their true nature and purpose, all in the protection represented by the garden.

Metaphysically, the "garden" is the illusion created by Time and Space, two phenomena which do not actually exist in the spiritual realm. Time and space were created to give the companions a reality in which they could change or progress from one state of being to a higher state by correcting and improving. Eventually, they would perceive themselves as having been born anew, or, using a biblical description from the Revelation, they would perceive their soiled garments to be clean again. Their transgressions against the very Source which gave them life would be resolved in time, and space gave them a place to be separate until they were ready to be one with the All-Knowing.

But once again the companions-to-be chose to do what they wanted, and they ate the fruit! The resulting knowledge caused them to feel immense guilt, so much so that they "hid from God," feeling they were "naked." The awareness of good and evil and the subsequent guilt made God's efforts to help them even more difficult. Now they were going to have to go even farther away from God's presence until they could feel redeemed enough to seek and abide in His/Her presence again (Rev. 7:14).

The author of Genesis subtly reveals this growing distance from God by changing His name as the companions continue to move farther away. Accordingly, man was first created by "God," but when he entered the physical world his body was made by the "Lord God" with whom he shared the garden. Finally, after the loss of the garden, he related to the divine as "Lord."

For a long time things got progressively worse. Cain and Abel could only relate to their creator through altar sacrifices. Eventually, the people could not even conduct their own altar sacrifices; it had to be done for them by an anointed one; a priest, prophet or holy man. Still later they wanted one of their members to be appointed king over them so he could tell them what to do (I Samuel, chap. 8). Their personal, direct relationship with the Creator was becoming blocked by layers of protective barriers, until the people no longer knew they were each meant to be direct, personal companions to the Creator. In fact, this was the principal crime that led to Jesus' being sentenced to death: he claimed to be the "Son of God," in personal touch with God, and God was his father! This claim was too much for the authorities to accept; no man was that closely related to God. This shows just how far away from their true nature man had come.

Let's return to the garden again. Since the souls had come to know what they had done and who they were by eating the forbidden fruit, it was imperative that their hiding from the Creator not go on forever. After all, they were supposed to become the companions of the Creator. And so, the fruit from the Tree of Life (representing unlimited access to the spirit, and therefore, immortality) was taken away from them and protected from them. They would no longer have unlimited access to life's "power source" as they had always had before this fall. Now they would have only as much life or spirit as they sought through attunement to the spirit while incarnate. The less they remained attuned to their true life Source, the more they had to consume what little of the *élan vital* they had. When it ran out, they could no longer sustain their bodies and they died, leaving them without a physical vehicles in which to manifest. In this way they were unable to make a permanent home in the third dimension as terrestrial beings, and were forced to experience and re-familiarize themselves with the other dimensions from which they had originally come.

Jesus and Reincarnation and Karma

"'But I tell you, Elijah has already come, and they did not recognize him, but have done to him everything they wished.' Then the disciples understood that he was talking to them about John the Baptist."
—Jesus, (Matthew 17:12, 13)

"And his disciples asked him, saying, 'Master, who did sin, this man, or his parents, that he was born blind?'"
—John 9:2 (For Jesus' disciples to even asked him such a question indicates that they were aware of karma and karmic rebirth.)

5. TO THE RESCUE!

The souls near the Earth but not involved in it were in a position to help the Earthbound souls. At first they entered straight into the Earth to help reawaken the others, but when they found themselves becoming distracted, confused and captivated by manifesting in form, they wisely decided to regroup and reconsider more carefully how they might achieve a rescue. It quickly became apparent that the physical dimension was a far more difficult problem than anyone had at first imagined. No matter how good one's intentions, once the transition from soul-in-consciousness to soul-in-substance was made, it was nearly impossible to retain an awareness of one's true nature. Substance was too consuming, and one couldn't just touch it and then leave it. To use an old Southern concept, it was like grabbing hold of a tar baby – once you touched it, it had a hold of you.

In some ways, entering physical form can be compared to entering a costume ball. In order to get in you have to put on a costume, and once in costume you and those around you begin to think of each other as being the image of the costumes. After playing this game long enough, you become so familiar with the costume reality that it becomes the dominant reality. You forget everyone is really a person in a costume. And, of course, to add to the confusion, the ball is very exciting, filled with lights, music, foods of all kinds, dancing and activities galore! Your entire focus becomes the ball, the costumes, the adventure; and the party seems to go on forever. But the longer you stay the more your costume wears away, until it is worn thin, the seams give way, and you can't use it any longer. Without a costume you must leave. If you want to return, you must find another costume. Then, you enter the party again. Before you know it, everything revolves around the ball and your efforts to stay at the ball – or return to it with a new costume. Everyone has by now forgotten that within the bodies are real souls, and beyond the physical world is an entire spiritual universe with a Creator who wants to share it.

Helping the souls at the "costume-ball" was not going to be easy. They were now so focused on the ball and the costumes that they could only be communicated with at the ball and in costume. The rescuing souls were going to have to risk getting themselves lost in order to communicate with the others. Ultimately, all the souls that touched the physical would have to experience the separation of consciousness and the blinding limitations of three-dimensional reality – and then somehow overcome it! There was simply no easy way in and out; one had to come to terms with it until no longer possessed by it.

To protect against the loss of the truth completely, the rescuing souls wove the truth about the companions and their predicament into the fabric of physical life, into its legends and myths, its art and symbols. Thus, when any lost soul sought beyond what he found in physical life, the real truth would be there for him or her to rediscover.

Three examples of how secret-meaning tales hold the treasures of this ancient truth are Sleeping Beauty, Snow White and Pinocchio. Each of these compelling tales has a theme based on the battle between good and evil for possession of an innocent person who wants only to live happily ever after. Despite all efforts to prevent it, the innocent one is killed by evil, but eventually comes to life again through the forces of good, and experiences the full measure of his or her dreams.

In Sleeping Beauty's tale, her marriage to the prince is doomed when she pricks her finger on a spinning wheel and dies, but the penalty is reduced from eternal death to "a deep sleep." Through the prince's efforts to free himself from the grips of evil and defeat the dragon, he is able to reach Sleeping Beauty and awaken her.

In Snow White's tale, her marriage to the prince is lost because she eats the apple that evil presents to her and dies; but she is not really dead, only in a deep sleep. After searching long and hard, the prince finally finds her deep in the forest and awakens her with a kiss.

In Pinocchio's tale we find a wooden boy who can become a real boy only if he proves himself worthy. In his efforts to live the way he should, Pinocchio falls prey to many of evil's distractions; each has a devastating effect on him, and the last challenge kills him. But because he was trying to save Geppetto's life rather than his own in those final minutes of life, he is granted the promise of the good fairy and comes alive again as a real boy.

In the tales of Sleeping Beauty and Snow White, the soul of a companion is symbolized by the beautiful, innocent princess. The prince symbolizes the mind of the companion. He is the companion's power to reason, understand, and perceive so that he can cut through the illusionary powers and darkness of evil and reunite with his soul. It is the light of understanding that shines through the darkness and reveals the truth. In these two tales the mind had to struggle with many powerful illusions before it could possess its soul.

Sleeping Beauty's loss of consciousness by pricking her finger while spinning on her spinning wheel is symbolic of the soul's entry into flesh and blood through the use of its free will (spinning its pattern). The evil fairy who predicts the coming doom and eventually grows into the fiery dragon who challenges the mind's efforts to revive the soul is the evil of self – self-glorification, self-aggrandizement, self-centeredness, and self-willfulness – all to the detriment of the soul.

We see this same evil power personified in the Stepmother-Queen of Snow White. "Mirror, mirror on the wall, who's the fairest of them all?" As we will see later in the legend of the Fallen Angels, this self-centered vanity is a major stumbling block to spiritual consciousness and true freedom.

In Pinocchio we have an even clearer picture of the companion's struggle. Pinocchio (the individual soul) cannot become a real companion and share the full meaning of companionship with his father (the heavenly father), who created him, until he comes to terms with his freedom to choose. Of course, his conscience shows him the way. Here, as well as in true life, concern for others is a major step in recovering from self-centered use of free will. Pinnocchio's selfless concern for Geppetto, resurrected him from death and transformed him into the boy he was always meant to be.

There are many fairy tales, myths and legends containing elements of the story of the companions. Inevitably they become the favorites.

Another tale is The Wizard of Oz. In this story the soul, as Dorothy, finds herself in a strange land far from home. In her quest to get back home she meets three aspects of herself that are lacking something: heart (the Tinman), mind (the Scarecrow), and courage or will (the Cowardly Lion). By following the path replete with trials, she arrives at the Wizard's castle only to find that the way home was within her all the time. So it is with the companions of God who are in the Earth. Of course, before we return, we have to take away the broom from the last remaining wicked witch, freeing the land of her tyranny!

Another story that we should consider before we move on is the legend of the Fallen Angels. Here we find the basic theme again, but with a curious twist.

In heaven there was an angel of such beauty and brilliance that he was called "The Morning Star." His name was Lucifer. Lucifer began to think that he was the most beautiful being in the heavens. He was so beautiful that he felt others should consider his nature and defer to it. He began to do as he pleased and encouraged others to follow him. All thought of the Universal, non-personified Creator that made him was lost, and he was pulling others away with him.

Once the rebellion was discovered, God brought forth his archangel, Michael, to throw Lucifer and his followers out of Heaven to protect it from any further rebellion. Michael threw them into Hell and Earth where they ruled until a Redeemer was sent to resurrect them to their former state.

A penance was decided upon by God and the other angels. Lucifer must subordinate his will to the will of God until he preferred God's will to his own. In addition, he must help those angels he encouraged to rebel by showing them his preference for God's will over his own. If this were done, the Morning Star would shine again in the heavens.

In this legend we have the whole story of the companions' struggle with free will and independent consciousness, though it is difficult to consider the lost companions as being symbolized by Lucifer and his fellow angels! But according to the secret teachings, they are the fallen angels, lost to their original purpose and nature through their own self-glorifying use of free will. But, even Lucifer was given life by God, and since God wishes that not one of His creations be lost forever, a way was prepared for all to return to their former place.

THE PASSAGE THROUGH THE REALM

Now the pattern for a soul involved in the Earth was set. It would sojourn in the third dimension in a human body living in time and space, physical form and duality. The realm would be "The Land of Choice," where each soul would be presented with those choices that would lead to the fulfillment of self, or those that would lead to the fulfillment of one's purpose with the Divine. It was hoped that the soul would apply itself to the positive choices that presented themselves in this unique realm, selecting good over evil, truth over falsehood, others' needs over one's wants, the harmony of the Whole over the pleasures of selfishness; and that the companion would then reach beyond self and seek again a conscious awareness of the Creator. All of this would require subduing the incompatible drives of one's free will and getting control over the forces and illusions of the physical world. Furthermore, the soul would have to meet the consequences of its own actions – healing the wounds it had inflicted on itself and others, righting the wrongs, and untying the fetters it had placed on itself and others.

By making the right choices and living more and more like a companion of the Creator, the soul could regain its previous consciousness and state. But it was a tremendously difficult task, requiring a very long time, as the Earth counts time. Many cycles of being in-the-body and in-the-spirit was required.

With each physical life came the opportunity to not only desire the former state of spirit consciousness and companionship with the Creator, but to actually live it through actions, thoughts – choosing the eternal over the temporary, harmony over discord, cooperation over rebellion, and the Universal over self. The more one chose the fruits of the spirit, the more one became the spirit again, freeing oneself of the possessive powers of the physical. Eventually, this would lead to a new awareness of actually being a soul manifesting a body rather than just a body.

With each death in the physical came the birth again into the spirit and the opportunity to reflect on how well the individual used the opportunities in its most recent incarnation. The memories and impressions left from the soul's incarnation gave it strength and encouragement for completing the task of the reunion. As one proved to itself that it not only desired the former state but actually lived it and chose it, one gained strength over its guilt and doubt, and came again into the presence of the all-knowing God, its Father/Mother and Companion.

Now that the passage through the difficult physical dimension and back to the Creator was established, there remained only for some soul to go through it and reach the other side. By doing so, this soul would make the way clear and easier for others to get through. But who would go first? Most of the lost ones were so busy with their own pursuits that they didn't even care about the passage. But many others longed to return home and regain their true place, yet they were doubtful, weak, and weary of the effort required. According to some of the secret teachings and those of Edgar Cayce, the first soul to volunteer to go through every trial, overcome every temptation, dispel every illusion, conquer every challenge and reach perfection was that soul we call Jesus of Nazareth.

THE FIRST BEGOTTEN SON
"No man has ascended up
to heaven but he that came
down from heaven, even the
Son of man..."
– Jesus Christ (John 3:13)

This soul entered the world of form and "dwelt among us," living through every phase of physical life. He did not accomplish this in one physical lifetime, as we are commonly led to believe, nor was he born perfect as some insist. He was born a human being, but he assumed a purpose and mission that made him very different from most humans. He lived like a normal person, experienced the same temptations, weaknesses and distractions that all humans experienced. But, through compliance with the Universal Law and the Father's Will, he overcame the physical world. Thus did this Soul regain its former state of consciousness, fulfilling its great purpose – showing the way to all who would choose to follow. By doing this, Jesus became the model, the way, the example (in Cayce's words, "the ensample") for all souls in and around the influences of Earth.

Not only did he do this in Earth, but according to Cayce, he did it with each planetary realm in this system! Thus, he perfected Mind (Mercury), Heart (Venus), Flesh (Earth), "madness" (Mars), strength (Jupiter), the force of change (Saturn), the psychic

(Uranus), the mystic (Neptune) and consciousness (Pluto).

Such a feat was not accomplished quickly or easily. He suffered; experiencing losses, broken hearts, deaths and confusion. According to Cayce, it was a process spanning some thirty incarnations, and hundreds of thousands of years. (I'll share more of this story in the chapter on Leila's soul journey.)

This is not to say that this great soul has not been on the Earth since that humble, yet profound, life in Palestine; quite the contrary. According to many sources, he continues to enter and help with the continuing rescue of the lost companions. According to Cayce, he manifests in the physical world in the same body that he resurrected. He no longer incarnates through birth. Of course, as we already know, this doesn't mean we will immediately recognize him, just as they didn't on the road to Emmaus (Luke 24:13-35) But, let's look at some of his incarnations as he perfected the way.

His first appearance, as Paul indicates (I Cor. 15:45), was as Adam in which he became a living soul and first experienced physical form, leading to the loss of God's presence and the pain of death. He came again as Enoch who walked and talked with God. In Adam he was not born of woman but created by God, yet through original sin came to know death. As Enoch, He was born in the normal way but did not experience death ("God took him," Gen 5:24).

He appeared again as Melchizedek ("priest of the most high God"), who was neither born nor died, greeting and blessing Abram in the desert (Gen. 14:18-20). Paul may be indicating his knowledge of this incarnation of Jesus in the following quote from Hebrews.

Whither the forerunner is for us entered, Jesus, made an high priest for ever after the order of Melchizedek. For this Melchizedek, king of Salem, priest of the most high God, who met Abraham returning from the slaughter of the kings, and blessed him...first being by interpretation King of righteousness, and after that also King of Salem, which is, King of peace; without father, without mother, without descent, having neither beginning of days, nor end of life; but made like unto the Son of God; abides a priest continually....And it is far more evident: for that after the similitude of Melchizedek there arises another priest, who is made, not after the law of a carnal commandment, but after the power of an endless life. (Hebrews 6:20-7:16)

Next he came as one of the sons of Jacob, subjected to all the influences of men and their activities. In this incarnation he did not possess supernatural powers, but held fast to that faith that the heavenly Father would be near even in the most desolate places. In this incarnation he was Joseph. He was sold by his brothers and taken into the land of the Pharaoh, alone and imprisoned, yet knowing the Father was always aware of him. This belief led to the opportunity to rise to a position of great power and influence by correctly interpreting the dream of Pharaoh. Eventually, Jacob became a savior to his brothers who had sold him away. (Gen. 37:23-45:28) This life was a major preparation for his entry as Jesus the Savior.

Even as Jesus he faced tests, first with the three temptations of the devil and then in the garden where he struggled with his personal desire not to experience the final test and God's desire that he do so. The last for him to overcome was death. Submission of his will and trust to the will and care of the Father was the way to victory over death. In passing through these tests he gained power over death and oneness with the Father.

To truly comprehend this accomplishment, we need to realize that his body was drained of all its natural fluids, blood, and water, and was dead for three days; yet, it came to life again. He walked, talked and ate (Luke 24:42-43) with this resurrected body.

According to Jesus' own teachings, it is the spirit that gives life, not the flesh. The absence of spirit is physical death and the presence of spirit gives life again, even to a three-day-dead body. Lazarus' body had been dead for a week when Jesus called Lazarus' soul to enter it again. For those souls who have come to believe only in the reality of this terrestrial world, these are impossible feats. But once one realizes that he is a spirit and the spirit lives continuously, then raising the empty three-dimensional vehicle with the spirit is easy to comprehend – well, easier. However, having knowledge of something and having the power that comes from true understanding of it are two different things. We can hear something and even believe in it, but we will rarely act as though we believe it unless we have personally experienced it.

Saying that we are the children of God and the eventual companions of God who have gone astray for a time, and that we are actually celestial beings of spirit, mind and soul with free will and independent consciousness is all very well, but really being such is entirely a different matter. In the experiences of the soul Jesus we can see how all phases of the fall from grace, the struggle with the distracting forces of self's will, the influences of the physical and the rise again to the original consciousness can be achieved – slowly, patiently, step by step, line upon line, "here a little, there a little" (as the Cayce readings encourage), and before you know it, you are there. This is not thinking or believing you are a celestial being or companion of the Creator, but actually being one.

THE LAND OF CHOICE

Hundreds of thousands of years have now passed since the companions first entered the Earth. In some ways it must seem as though the rescue has failed. As we look around the planet we still see hundreds of millions of souls who seem to have little awareness of their true nature, their true purpose for living. We see injustice, cruelty, war, violence, all kinds of suffering and deprivation. Yet, in the midst of all of this the rescue continues – quietly, soul by soul. It's as though there were two worlds here on Earth, one focused on the day-to-day activities of the physical planet, with its nations, cities, businesses, races, languages, religions, schools and endless activities; and another focused on the universal, timeless growth of the souls and their relationship with and awareness of the First Cause, the Creator, the Universal Consciousness. Amid the buying and selling, the building up and tearing down, the fighting and the loving, is a gentle, rising awareness of the brotherhood of all people and a sense of the spirit that survives the material.

There still remains the tendency to seek for solutions among the things of this world when it can only be found within the inner place of one's being. It is not outside among the many physical manifestations of this world, but within the consciousness of each soul. The physical world is not to be ignored; in fact, it plays a major part in the soul's resurrection, as we shall see.

6. The Lives of Leila, One Soul's Journey

Since Leila Evans died when she was only two and a half, we might well expect there would be very little story to tell. Actually, the real story begins with this little one's death. Had she lived, she would have been a close companion of Edgar Cayce's, who incarnated seven short months after her death. The doctors never knew exactly why Leila died. But her mother knew intuitively that she had slowly drifted away because the family situation had become less than ideal for a little girl, particularly this little girl.

Leila died August 24, 1876. Some sixty years later, 1936, a young woman walked into the offices of the then aging Edgar Cayce and asked if he would give her one of his now famous readings. Mr. Cayce didn't need to give a reading to know who this woman was – he would have recognized the soul of Leila anywhere – but the subsequent reading served to confirm it. She was indeed the same soul who would have been Cayce's older sister had she not died just before his birth. The reading went on to say that Leila withdrew from that brief incarnation because the situation in the home was indeed not what she had expected. The reading intimated that the souls of Leila and her parents may have made an agreement with one another prior to her incarnation concerning the kind of home atmosphere they would have together in their

Earthly life. Apparently, the setting was not as agreed upon and Leila left. Leila's expectations must have been very specific and emotionally vital for her to leave a family who so adored her, for their little angel, according to the readings, was the special one of the family. However, the soul in the role of the father was not living up to his part of the plan, and this so upset Leila that her soul wouldn't stay. The readings indicates that the father's drinking was disrupting this loving family, and ruining Leila's hopes for the new life. The readings then say, rather cryptically, that she "withdrew to the deeper meditation in the Mercurian environs."

This quoted comment refers to a frequently expressed concept in the Cayce readings concerning soul experiences between physical lifetimes as sojourns in the surrounding environments of our solar system, particularly the "environs" of the other planets in our system. As discussed earlier, souls don't actually live on the planets as we do in the third dimension, but rather within and about fourth and fifth dimensional environs of these planets. It's as though each planet and star has its unique realm of experience that attracts souls for specific purposes. Apparently, Leila withdrew to what we might call the fourth-dimension of the planet Mercury – not on the planet Mercury but within its fourth-dimensional influences. Obviously, in dimensions beyond the third, Mercury would be quite a different environ than we are capable of perceiving with carnal eyes. (It seems the astrologers have long known that the planets are far more than physical spheres in dark space [see Chapter 3], assigning each planet a special set of characteristics that influence us. Mercury has astrologically represented the mind.) Leila sought refuge from her disappointment by sojourning there for exactly one "full cycle," 33 years, before until returning to the environs of Earth to reincarnate on August 24, 1910 – this time under the name of Barbara Murray. ※ 2390

Again was her childhood home setting lacking in many ways, forcing her to make a decision as to whether she would endure the shortcomings in order to take advantage of the opportunities available through these new parents.

It was at the age of thirty that she sat next to the then 60-year-old Cayce, listening to his description of her soul's life, which seemed to have been going on forever. Remember, had she remained as Leila with her former family incarnation, she would have been his 63-year-old sister. Life is so amazing when viewed from ther perspective of the soul. Happily for us, the readings tell of her soul's life from the very beginning, a story that goes something like this...

Leila's soul was first conceived in the Mind of God, as were each of us. She was among numerous lights that appeared in the dark, when the "morning stars sang together in the heavens." It was the first dawn and she found herself awake and filled with wonder. In this early morning light her virgin consciousness would have been so near to the infinite, omnipotent mind of her Creator that the two were as one. Throughout this wondrous Presence were countless others like herself, yet each with a slightly different point-of-being in the Whole.

What "creatures" these would have been; like no other. They possessed the ultimate combination of consciousness and freedom. And within them were the innate urges of their Creator's desire for companionship and creativity, two celestially primal drives that would remain a driving force forever.

The angels must have looked upon these cosmic-toddlers with justifiable apprehension. Like celestial children they would have to learn to handle and value the treasures of this angelic home with care, but until they did learn what would the heavens be like? Chaos was a very real potential! It must have quickly become apparent to the angels that their home would never be the same again.

Flush with life, their minds ablaze with wonder and imbued with the essence of their Creator, these fledgling gods began to move, to touch, to seek out and look through the seemingly endless fathoms of the Cosmos. As a child would explore everything she found before her, Leila and the others peered into the many and varied mansions of their Father's house. Wonders upon wonders were to be found everywhere their young minds turned.

As with so many of us, Leila's wonder brought her into the environs of our present solar system. When she fully arrived here the Earth was still cooling and life was just beginning to stir in its waters and gases. This first appearance was not an incarnation of Leila's for there were no Earthly bodies to inhabit as we know them today. In this dawn of Earth's life she was more like a spirit in the breeze, a voice in the wind as it swept across the steaming waters – a voice foretelling of the coming of man.

But Earth was not the only planet she visited, neither was the third-dimension her primary level of consciousness. All the planets in this star system provided her with unique perspectives and opportunities in her young life. The entire universe with all its dimensions was hers to enjoy. By doing so, she would grow in understanding and come to be a true companion to the One who created her.

Leila's soul was not alone. In this childhood of the Sons and Daughters of God, she was among countless souls that turned their attention on this little part of the universe.

At this point in her celestial life, Leila was not a female spirit. Like all companions, she possessed both male and female sexual forces. Her nature of "form" could best be described as a consciousness which could, in moments, be very defined and unique, focusing-in on the minutest parts of manifested life, and at other moments could expand into the Universal Consciousness and perceive the Whole of Life. She was a microcosm of the Whole, a miniature of her Creator, a "chip off the old block." If we approached her, we would see how life was being expressed, perceived and experienced by this one point in the Whole.

This was Leila in the heavens, long before she made a home in the Earth plane.

On one of her early visits to Earth, she and the group of souls with whom she was traveling saw a strangely different quality in many of the souls who had been sojourning near the environs of Earth. They appeared to be changing: they were more dense and heavy; their consciousness seemed narrower, less universal. As she and her companions studied this phenomenon they realized that the other souls were gradually moving so deeply into the Earth's dimension that they were separating from the rest of life, taking on the shapes and dimensions of this new world, causing them to lose awareness of the other dimensions and the higher, finer aspects of their own being. They were no longer just visiting this world; they were actually beginning to look like the animals indigenous to Earth – they had feathers, scales, horns and other appendages. They were totally new creatures – terrestrial and heavy, and communication with them became increasingly difficult.

To her amazement, they had developed a hierarchy among themselves, setting some souls above others, something that was totally alien to the heavenly spheres where they were all children of the same family and parentage; equals.

Perhaps the most astonishing change was that the souls who were now leading these terrestrial groups were expounding a belief that there actually was no central, universal consciousness to whom they could remain attuned; that in fact their source of life was not a celestial Creator of love and joy, but simply the impersonal force of organic, material life. Each soul was encouraged to take what it wanted from life with little regard for others and no regard for the Whole of life. Successful survivors deserved to live better and off the labor of the others because it would improve the race. Power, superiority, force, strength and survival of the fittest were among their many new beliefs.

Leila and her companions knew this was nonsense. They reasoned that some great distortion of perception had apparently come over these souls, and in order to see the truth again they needed to regain their finer nature and form. However, in order for Leila and her group to reach these souls, they were going to have to move deeper into the Earth's dimensions themselves – a move very few of them wanted to make – yet they couldn't just leave these lost souls in such a ridiculous state of awareness. After much reflection, Leila and her companions felt sure they could maintain their spiritual consciousness while communicating with these terrestrial ones.

The plan was to first approach those who were the least affected by the Earth's physical dimension, re-awaken them to the truth, and convince them to convey to the others that they were heading in the wrong direction and needed to turn around, returning to the higher dimensions of life and consciousness.

Though Leila had visited Earth before, this was to be her first sojourn among its unique realms. However, she was not in a body like the ones we occupy today. She, and those who came with her, made themselves known to the terrestrial souls by projecting three-dimensional images of themselves into the Earth's dimension using light, much in the way we create a hologram. At first Leila's image was much like a sphere of illuminated consciousness from which her thoughts could be conveyed to the terrestrial souls. But when it became apparent that the terrestrial souls were too three-dimensionally focused to relate to these images, Leila and her companions began to project a form that approached the shape of our bodies today, only much lighter and less dense, still very much like a hologram formed by light but with increasing definition.

Using this image-form she began to sojourn for the first time in what was to become the continent of Atlantis. Here many souls were living in various degrees of solidity and awareness. Since Leila retained her attunement to the Universal Consciousness, she was considered to be a goddess. Many came to her for guidance and help in understanding what was happening to them and their companions, but she also met with strong, aggressive challenges from the leaders of the terrestrially bound souls. They challenged everything she and her companions held to be true about the Universal One, the higher dimensions and our true purposes for being.

It quickly became apparent that this transformation in consciousness was going to take much longer than originally expected. The terrestrially possessed companions were far more involved in this world than had first been suspected. In fact, many of them were actually seeking to build colonies here and sojourn among the planet's trees, mountains, and waters indefinitely, which might have been completely compatible with the Creator if they had not also been developing an idolized interest in themselves and their own desires without any regard for others and the Universal Forces.

This self-seeking energy would prove to be the first evil, the first sin, and the followers and supporters of this self-centered movement would become known as "The Children of Darkness" because their paths led toward the abyss of separation and loss of contact with the Creator. Prior to these changes there had been only One Force. Now there were two; the second an evil that mounted life for its own purposes, destroying everything in its way. The loss of contact with any holistic source and interconnection to life, combined with the new paradigm reflected in the principles of "survival of the fittest," established an entirely new and inherently destructive dimension of consciousness.

Unfortunately, self-seeking was not the sole possession of the terrestrially bound souls. Every free-willed companion had within it the potential to begin seeking its own way without concern for the effect on others and the Whole. Free will and independent consciousness were godly gifts, yet with just the slightest shift in intent these sublime wonders of the fledgling gods became weapons of devils. Each of the companions had to struggle to subdue their self-only desires in order to remain in harmony with the Whole and the other companions.

Leila struggled hard to maintain her attunement and to aid those who sought her guidance and counsel, but she could feel herself assuming more and more the substance of the Earth, becoming heavier; and as she battled with the terrestrial leaders, she found herself becoming more willful and determined to force her views upon them. This righteous and well-meaning desire was subtly giving strength to forces of self-interest, but unlike some of her fellow companions, Leila perceived the effects of willfulness, and resisted.

Her name was now Asamee. Hers was not exactly an individual name as we have today; rather, it was the collective name for a line of souls, all of whom were called "Asamee." Individuality was not near what it has become today. Differentiating one soul from another wasn't done; all were still very much one. Those who felt as she did about life and consciousness were called "The Children of the Law of One." This name had come to them because of their insistence that there was only One Force in the universe, and souls were the children of the One. They also taught "The Law of the One," which included a principle that actions naturally produce reactions, an idea that the terrestrials considered ridiculous and just another attempt to keep them from doing whatever they wanted.

According to the Cayce readings, one of the souls who was with Asamee in these times was called Amilius. This soul would later become known as Jesus of Nazareth, savior of the world. His story weaves in and out of Leila's and is a fascinating one in itself. Cayce said that in these very early times on the planet, Amilius perceived the disastrous change that had come over his fellow souls, resulting in the terrestrial ones, and came to the conclusion that things had gotten beyond the level of a brief flirtation with the Earth. It was now time, he felt, to develop a much more long-term plan for dealing with the situation. On this point, many of the Children of the Law of One disagreed or had other ideas about how better to deal with the problem. Thus, for the first time, a difference of opinion arose within the ranks of the Children. Amilius, his intentions pure and his vision clear, was clearly attuned to the Universal Consciousness. Because of this, most of the Children supported his perceptions, some begrudgingly, others wholeheartedly, but of course, some resisted them strongly.

Amilius perceived that if this loss of celestial consciousness could happen to one soul, it could happen to any soul; therefore, the problem needed to be faced; the temptation needed to be overcome, not avoided. Furthermore, the root of the problem was not the Earth and its unique form of life, but the struggle within each soul to learn to use its godliness in such a way as to be all it was meant to be and yet not destroy itself and other life in the process. Key to this problem was the sense of separation a soul felt as it became more self-conscious and less universally conscious. This sense of separation, which resulted in a loss of purpose and identity with anything or anyone, occurred in the celestial realms as well as in the Earth, though more accentuated in the latter. Therefore, it was assumed the Earth was the best place to conquer it.

Amilius was making a commitment to enter the Earth and live among the lost ones to somehow overcome its destructive influences. He believed if self-consciousness and its resulting sense of separation could be overcome, it could be overcome here as well as anywhere else. And once overcome, it would no longer have any power over the Children, the future companions of God; they would know the truth and they would be free.

Some among Amilius' group wanted to leave these Earthlings to wallow in their own sins and delusions. Others doubted their own ability to resist the temptations that had so possessed the lost souls. For in addition to dealing with this problem of one's own inner temptations and struggles, they were going to have to deal with the terrestrial souls who had now become very aggressive and lawless. To attempt to live among them was not only spiritually, mentally and emotionally dangerous, it was physically dangerous. Some of the Children also pointed out that there were many complications involved in this Earth problem, so many complexities and complications that a real solution might well be impossible. Perhaps they would just be throwing good souls after bad if they attempted to enter and subdue this world.

With all of these hazards in mind and in spite of much bickering among the Children, Asamee and her fellow souls, including Amilius, began to set up a system whereby the lost ones could regain their heavenly consciousness, and along with the Children of the Law of One, learn to overcome their potential for evil. It was a grand endeavor, filled with that spirit that is only found in the faithful, the hopeful, the positive ones. Little did they know just how formidable their adversary was, both the inner and outer.

First on their list was to prepare a new physical form that would allow the companions of God to sojourn in the Earth with some semblance of their true, spiritual nature. Their animal-like forms were totally ill-suited for spiritual endeavors and actually added to their problems with perception and understanding. As companions of the Creator, they needed a physical form that suited their particular spiritual characteristics and yet was based on sound principles for functioning well in the third-dimension.

Furthermore, their sexual oneness had been eroded by the natural duality of the planet, causing them to accentuate one aspect of their sexual forces (male or female) and subdue the other (the respective male or female opposite). No longer were they united, androgynous beings; they were now either predominantly masculine or feminine in their appearance and energy. Physically, then, their new Earthly form would need to reflect these changes by being either male or female. Asamee and her fellow "double-sexed" companions began the work of creating forms for these souls, male and female, separating their double-sexed natures into single-sexed physical projections, Amilius being the first to completely achieve this.

The physical setting for all of these struggles and the subsequent work and commitment was Atlantis. Many souls were involved, and Leila interacted with most of them, their lives weaving in and out of hers throughout her incarnations In some cases, they built strong, lasting relationships that were forever a blessing to them. In other cases, they built disagreements, misunderstandings and distrust that haunted them whenever their paths crossed.

As this work continued, Leila withdrew from the Earth to prepare herself to be a channel through which the Children could enter into the new human bodies. She chose to accentuate her feminine forces and subdue her masculine, and throughout her many incarnations never changed her mind, remaining female in each.

These early periods in the Earth had gone on for an enormously long time. In Earth time, the activities in Atlantis lasted some 200,000 years. During the last 50,000 years the huge continent had broken into several islands from violent Earthquakes. Leila had sojourned here as Asamee for much of the early period and was preparing to return to Earth as the last of Atlantis sank into the sea and a new era began.

This would be her first true incarnation in that she was actually going to enter and live in a physical body, a female body, for the first time. It was not a haphazard event. Many of the souls with whom she had worked in Atlantis were already in the Earth preparing for her incarnation.

Conditions in the Earth had changed dramatically. En masse the souls had entered, preparing for generations of incarnations that were to be a part of this new world; a joyful solution, it was hoped.

In five different regions, in five different races, in five different nations the souls entered, each group manifesting a unique characteristic of their celestial nature and each responsible for maintaining and enlightening the physical world with that celestial aspect while the cycles of Earth-life moved toward their destiny.

[margin note: Five Races]

Leila was among those souls charged with developing the white race. Their original center was in the Caucasus Mountains, though many of them migrated into what today would be called northern Africa, Egypt, eastern Asia and Europe.

In Egypt, the high-priest Ra Ta, and several others working closely with him, were preparing for Leila's entry. Hers was to be a very special event for she had the potential to manifest the optimal characteristics of a true, pure, human-type physical body.

Many of the bodies in all races were contaminated and distorted by animal characteristics that lingered from the early days of the terrestrial ones. To produce a perfect form for the companions, one had to use the natural laws of the Earth's genetics combined with a clear mental image of the desired result... and then hope that the soul who inhabited the body possessed the same image and could maintain it long enough to manifest it firmly in physical form! Even then, the new creation could end up sexually mingling with another body that wasn't as purely human, mixing it with stronger animal characteristics, and ruin everything.

These were unusual times. There were no families, no parents, no laws – just millions and millions of souls in varying degrees of consciousness, with different motives and desires, and different physical bodies. The celestially attuned companions were living in human-like terrestrial forms, and though their proximity to the lost ones helped awaken many, it also helped to lower the awareness of the celestial ones.

Despite the temptations and difficulties, Ra Ta and his co-workers had prepared themselves and their bodies carefully. Among themselves they had selected two who were genetically, as well as mentally and spiritually, the best. These had been developed, preserved and finally brought together for the conception of a third body, one that would even better the parent bodies.

Leila had also well prepared herself. She had sojourned in the celestial environs with as pure an attunement to the Universal One as she could possibly manage. Her attunement was no longer what it had once been in the early morning moments after the original creation, where her life and awareness were one with All life. Too much had come between her and the deep stillness of the Universal One, but it was an attunement sufficient to make her a rare soul among Earth-bound souls and to bring a glimpse to others of what it had been like to be a morning star in that now distant dawn.

Ra Ta anxiously watched as the newborn was being received from the womb, and as it was being cleansed and prepared for presentation. His eyes searched for the tell-tale signs of beastliness or celestialness and the true characteristics of a pure human form. Again and again he scanned every detail of her body. Nothing, absolutely nothing was distorted or contaminated; she was truly human. Clear sharp eyes, pure skin, very little hair – the priest could hardly believe his eyes. She was the perfect human form for the heavenly souls to use during their incarnations in the new world. As he pulled away to reflect on the meaning and potential of the event, the others with him pushed their way in to see for themselves.

As mentioned briefly, the celestially aware companions entered in five different races. This was originally accomplished more in consciousness than in form, for their bodies did not immediately reflect true, pure human qualities but had to be developed toward this aim. At this early stage in man's entry into the Earth, human qualities were more mental images than physical forms, and in order to convert them into physical reality, it was essential to work within the laws of evolution and genetics native to the earth.

Ra Ta and his companions had finally achieved the perfected white body (originating in the Caucus and Carpathian areas, perfected in Egypt). The red had already been perfected (Atlantis and North America), as well as the brown (Lemuria and the Andes), the black (Sudan and Congo) and the yellow (Gobi area). Leila had been the soul that entered this first purely Caucasian body. Her new name, appropriate, was Tar Ello, "body of light." It was a high achievement for Leila. She gave hope and inspiration to many through her beautiful reflection of one of the five aspects of the heavenly "form." Man was no longer a beast of the world, but a descendant from another world above; a beautiful descendant. Now the work of the ascension was ahead of them, the return to their life "before the world was."

Though Tar Ello had accomplished much in achieving her first flesh body, it would prove to be a very difficult incarnation for her. She was looked upon with awe and reverence, and viewed and judged by her outer form more than her inner spirit. She naturally felt special, different and more alone than she had ever felt in the higher dimensions. Even some of her closest companions in the spirit were now so in awe of her that they set her above themselves, no longer swapping counsel and support, but expecting all the wisdom and strength to come from her alone. Others, who had been her friends and colleagues in the Atlantian sojourn, now resented her new physical superiority, feeling that she no more deserved such an honor than they.

Leila longed for the early times when no soul was greater than another and all shared together as equals and companions. On Earth everything was measured and judged by appearance, position and power. It was a lonely place to live, each within one's own body, separated from the others and measured by outer qualities and segregated accordingly.

Ra Ta perceived the girl's sadness, though ever so subtle it was, for she kept her mission above her personal needs. He encouraged her to take part in the ceremonies of the temples and find comfort in prayer and meditation. Ax-Tell and his son Ax-Tellus, both remnants of the Atlantian Civilization and members of the perfected red race, had long understood the problems of loneliness and separation in the new world. Seeing this same feeling in the eyes of this little white child and in so many others, they encouraged the high-priest Ra Ta and the king of the land, Ararat, to consider a new living arrangement for souls while incarnate in the Earth. Instead of living in medium to large groups, their plan was that each group would break into small sub-groups consisting of one male and one female whose offspring lived with them. Together they would form a support group for each of their members, their own flesh and blood the bonding force. It was the beginning of the nuclear family, as we know it, and the sense of support that came from being someone's child, sibling, or parent. This structure would also reflect the heavenly realm where the children of the father-mother God companioned in a close, nurturing environment.

It was an excellent idea, but Tar Ello was a temple virgin and there was no way Ra Ta was going to agree to allow her to live in a separate dwelling with her natural parents amid all the other souls of mixed blood and morality; this world was still too savage and beastly for that. She was too rare, too special. But those close to Tar Ello knew she carried a deep sadness and loneliness with her and she would not be the perfect temple priestess Ra Ta wanted. Nevertheless, she struggled hard to maintain her attunement to the Universal One and carried out her daily work to the best of her ability.

She continued to help make flesh a temporary home for spirit, drawing inspiration and guidance from her temple studies and duties and the many teachers and guides associated with the effort. One of these guides was Hermes, called by many the "Thrice Majestic One." He was, in fact, the soul who had been called Amilius in Atlantis. Continuing his work toward resurrecting the Earth-bound souls to their former state in the heavens, he was now here in Ancient Egypt among the Children who also worked toward such an end. As it is commonly known among the students of mystery today, Hermes was the major influence behind the building of the Pyramids. Since the descent of the souls was going to take them deep into the world of matter and physical reality, these monuments were built as reminders of the former realms that still lie beyond physical death. But they were more than monuments in those early days. Leila and her fellow Children of the One used some of these structures for their initiations into the true realities and purposes for life; truths that were fast becoming myths and legends. Through her close relationship with Ra Ta and his close relationship with Hermes, she continued to be involved with this great soul and His destiny.

Unfortunately, after the death of Ra Ta, who had become her inspiration and strength, Tar Ello fell from the high pedestal she had so sincerely accepted. Eventually, she left the temple to become the companion of Exderenemus, another remnant of Atlantis, and a soul with whom she would companion in many of her incarnations.

These dramatic changes in Tar Ello's life and position astonished those who worshipped her and caused those who resented her to take every opportunity to discredit her. All of this left Leila's soul deeply distressed. What had begun as a grand endeavor was ending in a purposeless mess. She withdrew from her body, from this place of sadness, and sought to rid herself of the memory of the whole experience. She withdrew to the realms of Saturn, and there purged herself of all remnants of the flesh. From here she withdrew even further from Earth, her spirit rising higher and higher until she could feel the light of the Universal One fill her being and purge her of her

Earthly dross, leaving it to die. Here in the heavenly spheres she bathed and rejuvenated herself until once again she and her Creator were in touch with each other.

As Earth keeps time, it wasn't long before the soul of the priest Ra Ta and Leila's other companions beckoned her to join them in another visit to the environs of Earth and yet another attempt at overcoming its peculiar influences while helping the terrestially bound souls reawaken themselves. It was too much a part of Leila's deepest wishes for her to refuse this goodwill mission, and since the Earth afforded her the opportunity to mend her disappointing sojourn in Egypt, she readily accepted the challenge. Off she went, revitalized and ready to make all aright.

Together with her little band of like-minded souls, Leila lived through many, many lifetimes in the Earth and in the realms beyond. Members of this loose-knit band were not always in agreement with each other or even considerate to one another, but, as is so often true of families, they were a unit, even at times, a team. One of their most significant incarnations came during the time of Christ.

In this incarnation Leila and Ra Ta were brother and sister. Her name was Nimmuo and his was Lucius. Both were prominent members of the church at Laodicea. The setting, as many of us know, was the Holy Land during the occupation of the Roman Legions. That particular portion of Asia had been under the control and supervision of the Roman Empire for a very long time, their presence and power permeating every aspect of life in these regions.

Nimmuo's father was of Roman descent and had two wives, one Grecian and one Jewish. Nimmuo was the child of the Greek mother while her brother Lucius was the son of the Jewish mother. Since the Romans always made attempts to put in authority any locals who showed the potential for having sympathy with the needs and demands of the Empire and who could be helpful in making activities with the local people more harmonious, her Roman-born father and, therefore, she and her family, enjoyed the support of Rome. For very practical reasons the armies of Rome did not want trouble with the people they conquered; they simply couldn't afford to keep expending any more of their resources governing these distant lands. Because of these practical needs and their policy of working with and supporting local people who showed signs of peaceful co-existence with them, Nimmuo's family was given many financial and personal freedoms that were rare in those times. Her father, with his Jewish wife and close connections with the Jewish churches in the North, was considered to be of great benefit to the Empire as a friend so that even their Jewish church profited. Nevertheless, Nimmuo and her family held tightly to the tenets and morals of their Hebrew faith, and though they interacted with the Roman leaders, shunned the lewdness and immorality the Romans brought to the Holy Land.

As the activities and teachings of Jesus reached their homeland in the North, the family began to come under their influence. To the Children of the Law of One, Jesus' teachings were a balm to their weary souls and a beacon pointing the way to a forgotten consciousness and life. And when his blossoming ministry abruptly changed during the periods of Jesus' trial and the Crucifixion, and then the subsequent reports that spread across the land as to what actually happened in the last hour of the Crucifixion, the reports of His rising again three days later and meeting with the disciples at the Sea of Tiberius, the entire family was caught up in wonderment and interest.

So Nimmuo, then barely sixteen years old, and her brother, who was now a leading minister in their church, set off to the south to learn everything they could about these reports. Nimmuo wanted to meet and talk with everyone who had come in contact with the Master. Because she and her brother traveled under the protection and support of the Romans, many along the way were skeptical of their true faith and loyalty to Israel and the Master's teachings. However, the sincerity and faithfulness of these two northerners was genuine and quickly perceived by the people they visited who shared with them the many stories about the Master's life and teachings.

They journeyed through the Holy Land, across the Sea of Galilee, down to those lands in Jordan through Perea to Bethany and the house of Martha, Mary and Lazarus, and then into the City of Jerusalem itself. They met Mary the Mother of Jesus and the rest of the family that had gathered under John's roof as he had been instructed from the Cross.

In Bethany they heard the story about Mary Magdalene's cleansing from her sins and Martha's devotion and tireless efforts to care for everyone's needs. Straight from Lazarus himself they heard about his death and his feelings and consciousness during the four days that his dead body lay in the tomb, and what it was like in the realms between Earth-life and Spirit-Life – how he had heard and felt the movement within himself when the Voice called, "Lazarus, come forth!"

All this affected Nimmuo to her very soul, making contact with those old sensations when she had been so close to her Creator, and leaving an imprint on her soul-memory forever.

She listened to the reports of how people had been healed by the laying on of His hands or merely His word spoken; how they had eaten bread that had been created by the word of the Teacher. She and her brother were forever changed by the recounting of these experiences which kept them in rapt attention over and over again. Hearing these reports first-hand meant that Nimmuo and Lucius would be able to share these reports in great detail with their family, friends and church members back in Laodicea who until now had had to settle for translations through many tongues – meaning that much was always lost in the process.

However, these times of enlightenment and awakening were not to pass peacefully. The Romans began to move against this growing new group that they considered to be nothing more than troublemakers. Nimmuo was present at one such event when James, the brother of Jesus, was chosen as head of the new church along with Peter. She witnessed how the other James and his brother John, the sons of Zebedee, had so stirred the spirit of the crowds that the Romans became afraid of the mass meeting and attacked with swords drawn, killing John's brother and many others during the riot, and eventually exiling John to Patmos. These two sons of Zebedee had long been called "the sons of thunder" and the Romans had had enough of them. From this moment on the followers of the humble Nazarene would be persecuted by the authorities.

With the scattering of the disciples and friends, Nimmuo and her brother returned to Laodicea and the other churches of the north. Here they both grew in power and position because of their travels, knowledge, and understanding about this great event. Deep within Nimmuo she felt the essence of those things she heard in the homes of Mary, Martha, Lazarus and the Mother. As so often in her previous lives, her soul yearned for the Spirit, for that soothing sense of the Divine Presence that she had always loved. Now, amid all the daily activities of this world and its limited perspective on life, she applied herself to the work that had begun many thousands of years earlier in that lost and forgotten land of Atlantis.

Remember, everyone with whom she presently associated had been involved with her in Atlantis and Egypt, and several lifetimes in between. Amilius, that soul who had been so attuned in the early periods that he committed himself to the rescue of the lost souls, was the very person they now called Jesus. In this Divine incarnation He prepared the final phase of salvation for all Earth-bound souls. He and the heavenly Father were one throughout this life; not separate. This showed to all who could still see with their spiritual, celestial eyes that reunion with the Creator could be done, thereby making it easier for others to do also. His words came from beyond the present world from the Universal Consciousness, our heavenly Father who created us in the very beginning:

"You are not of this world." (John 3:12)

"Is it not written in your laws that you are gods? Yet you say... 'Thou blasphemest' because I say I am the Son of God." (John 10:30-36)

"In my Father's house are many mansions... I go to prepare a place for you...And where I go you know, and you know the way." (John 14:2-4)

"I came forth from the Father and came into the world, now I leave the world and go to the Father." (John 16:28)

"No one has ascended up to heaven but he that came down from heaven..." (John 3:13)

These words and the stories she heard on her journey through Jesus' homelands filled Nimmuo's soul with a new fervor and determination to continue with the work. Along with her brother and many others, she ministered to the needs of the people, particularly those involved in the church at Leodicea. And when the church was nearly destroyed from within by a severe difference of opinion on how best to judge what was right and what was wrong, Nimmuo's serene and patient counsel kept the church from dividing in two. She seemed to sense the inner meaning of the teachings and never got lost in the many surface interpretations and dogmas to which man so often binds others once they are created.

This was not an easy time for this soul. She was surrounded by the very same souls who had seen her fall in Egypt, and many of them doubted her new-found inspiration, suspecting she would once again let them down. But they underestimated her determination to make things right with all those souls she had once failed. This was her opportunity and she seized it, snatching victory from out of the mouth of defeat. With all the wisdom and strength within her, she rose to the occasion and many other souls rose a little higher because of her. This was her soul's finest hours.

She lived a long and fulfilling life and withdrew to the peace of the heavenly environs for a lengthy period of meditation, letting the truths of that incarnation permeate deeply into her consciousness. She was a far wiser child of God than the one who taught in Atlantis. She had seen the face of the beast and tamed it, at least most of it. But there was a little more yet to deal with, as she would soon see.

After sojourning in the heavens for many Earth years, the soul of Leila returned for an incarnation that was most uncharacteristic. The Earth was now a major center of physical activity and densely populated. All of life and the universe were now viewed almost totally from a physical perspective. The history of the Earth established and supported the concept of physical reality being the only certain reality, and nearly everyone lived by this guiding concept. Business and commerce, religion and government, love and money had all become the powerful structures in which most lived. Into this world, so very different from that earlier world, the soul of Leila incarnated as one of the daughters of a wealthy and prominent Englishman. Her name was Marge Olglethorp. She learned her role well and even enjoyed it. Parasols, long, whirling hoop skirts, fancy buggies and parties with all kinds of foods and beverages were the style of the day. Life was just a bowl of cherries, ripe for the eating and enjoying. Amazingly, Leila, as Marge, took to this fun little lifetime quite well. No great mission beyond pomp and pleasure; no great challenges to overcome beyond style and good taste – life was to be lived to its fullest.

On one of the family's journeys to America, Marge found herself caught-up in the role of being a southern belle and was well received by the ladies and gentlemen of this land of willows and moss, huge plantations and wealth beyond measure. Here she lived the life of a Georgia peach, with that special touch of breeding that is forever English. Ra Ta was not involved in this lifetime, but Exderenemus, her husband in Ancient Egypt, was. In fact, he had incarnated with her in the Palestine lifetime when she was Nimmuo, but the two of them did not develop a very close relationship in that life. In the present incarnation in England and Southern America a terrible disagreement ended their relationship with such bitterness that they would of necessity face it again in a future incarnation.

How did this carefree lifetime become part of the experience of a soul who was once the goddess of Atlantis, the perfection of Ancient Egypt and a minister of Laodicea? The Eastern teachings of reincarnation include a concept that souls live a carefree incarnation about every six incarnations – a vacation, if you will, from the main work of spiritual resurrection. Perhaps the soul of Leila was enjoying a much needed break from her many serious lifetimes of devotion, trial and hard lessons learned.

It was after her incarnation as Marge that she reincarnated as the Leila Cayce of the beginning of our story, and subsequently reincarnated as Barbara Murray, the lady who found herself sitting that day some 30 years later next to the "sleeping prophet" Edgar Cayce, as he had been called in one biography. Barbara was a serene, elegant woman who devoted much of her time and energy to the work of Edgar Cayce, who, not surprisingly, was the reincarnation of the soul who had been Ra Ta in Ancient Egypt and her brother Lucius in Palestine. In the present lifetime, Barbara married Exderenemus again, now called Ryan Simons. The Cayce reading warned them not to let this relationship end like it had in their previous life together. Amilius was now their Christ, having become one with the Father again and resurrected to prepare a place for them and each and everyone of us. The three of them, Barbara, Ryan, and Edgar Cayce, had long ago dedicated themselves and their lives to this soul they had known so closely throughout His lifetimes and His Earthly mission. They continued to live and teach the mystery that we are all celestial beings descended from our original heavenly kingdom through a long and arduous journey in this realm of physical reality, and destined to return from whence we came.

Josephus on Reincarnation
—Jewish historian who lived around the time of Jesus

"All pure and holy spirits live on in heavenly places, and in course of time they are again sent down to inhabit righteous bodies."

7. PAST LIVES & PRESENT RELATIONSHIPS

We are like rivers. On the surface we are all shiny and clear, shimmering with freshness and life, but deep within us run powerful unseen currents of soul-memories and desires. These deep currents are the cumulative effects of ages of soul-life and many incarnations in the Earth. They cause us to love one person and despise another; to feel wonderful vibrations with a particular individual in one aspect of our lives only to feel awkward and uncomfortable with that same person in another aspect of our lives. Patterns and habits have formed deep within our inner-consciousness and shape the way we interact with people around us.

Everyone involved in our present lives was very likely involved in our past lives. Actually, it is likely they have been involved in many of our past lives. Our parents, brothers and sisters, spouses, children, friends, colleagues, bosses and employees, and even our enemies began sharing life with us long before the present lifetime.

The effects of these many past-life experiences are reflected in the circumstances that now surround our present relationships. The soul's memories of past-life activities with others shape our innate reactions to them. Of course, their memories of our past-life actions influence how they react to us. Through the same eyes that the personality sees life, the soul sees it, but the soul looks with a memory covering centuries of passion and adventure, caring and love, hatred and revenge, doubt and fear. When we feel a seemingly unfounded fondness for another person, it is very likely due to soul memory of the positive role he or she played in our past lives. On the other hand, when we react with what seems to be an unfounded revulsion or hatred towards another person, you can be pretty sure it is because the soul recalls their past actions against us or our loved ones.

However, the influences of past-life actions are rarely so clear cut. Often those with whom we have had many good lives and relationships are the same people with whom we have had many problems and disagreements, a mix of "good" and "bad karma," so to speak. In fact, it's rare that a past-life relationship has every aspect of life in good, clear focus. Those positive, well-developed aspects from our past lives will give us much pleasure and support in the present. Conversely, those aspects which we did not have in proper focus will give us opportunities for pain and growth in present relationships. Avoiding these influences is simply not possible. Whether we like it or not, the Universal Law of Karma constantly brings before each of us the meeting of our past use of free will and consciousness. Thus, what we have done to other souls and they have done to us is reflected in the circumstances surrounding our present relationships and the basic, innate urges, attitudes and emotions we feel toward each other.

SOUL GROUPS

These basic ideas of past relationships and their present influences are not only true of individual relationships but also of group relationships. From the beginning our souls have tended to travel together in groups, and the very act of traveling together for such long periods creates forces of attraction that help to maintain and build on these group relationships. Nearly all souls on the planet today were together in past ages of human history. As a result, the relationships among the peoples of the world today are a reflection of their past activities with each other.

The souls who came in to this planetary system and entered the realms of consciousness associated with this region of the cosmos comprise our largest soul group. This group can then be divided into the subgroups we call "the generations," containing souls who move through the natural cycles of Earth life together, which can be further divided into the various nations, cultures, races, religions, etc., that have formed during ages of interaction together. Within these groups are the subgroups of souls who share similar philosophies, ideas, purposes, aspirations and attitudes. From here the soul groups further divide into the many smaller groups of personal relationships: communities, families, businesses, teams, schools and so on.

Soul groups create an affinity among their members by not only the cumulative experiences they share, but also through their collective memory of how life has been for them and what they have come to mutually desire out of it. In a manner of speaking, such groups form a distinct collective consciousness and spirit, much like the souls who gave us "the spirit of '76," reflecting that soul group's mutual hopes, attitudes, purposes and memories.

Soul groups are neither rigid nor static. Any individual soul can use its free will to seek an experience in another group. There are many cases of souls changing political allegiance, race, or religion from one lifetime to another. Neither do the generations incarnate in strict, rigid patterns. A member of one generation may enter again with another generation. For example, two members of a family group who were father and son in one life may change positions and become son and father in another, or grandfather and grandson. They may even choose to be in the same generation in an incarnation as brothers, for example. However, they may choose not to be in the same family again.

Although soul groups are fairly well established and have significant pull on the individuals within them, they do not have greater influence than an individual soul's will to change.

Generally, however, soul groups cycle in and out of the Earth together and, therefore, at approximately the same time. (I am speaking in eras and ages, not days or years.) This is particularly evident in the past-life readings, as they are called, of Edgar Cayce. Many of them were for souls who fell into one of two major soul groups and naturally followed their cycles of incarnation. Notice in the following listing that the two groups mentioned were sometimes in the Earth at the same periods, but in different locations, not surprisingly. Edgar Cayce and those who worked closely with him also traveled with one of these two groups.

THE INCARNATIONS OF TWO MAJOR SOUL GROUPS

Group l:
Early Atlantis
Early Ancient Egypt
Lydia/Persia (during the time of Croesus I, II)
Palestine (during the time of Christ)
The Crusades
Colonial America

Group 2:
  Late Atlantis
  Late Ancient Egypt
  Early Greece
  Rome (during the time of Christ)
  France (during the time of Louis XIV, XV, XVI)
  The American Civil War

Of course, these are only the most significant incarnations for these souls; they would most probably have incarnated many more times than the list indicates. There were also other incarnation-sequences given, but the majority of the readings were for souls who typically cycled with one of these two major groups. We should also take a look at.some significant exceptions to this pattern. Some souls did not always incarnate with their group, choosing instead to skip a cycle or enter with another group, though they usually rejoined their original group eventually. Others, though cycling into the Earth-plane with their group, did not actually incarnate, i.e., did not enter into a body; rather they stayed in the spirit and helped from a higher vantage point while the others incarnated. One example of this comes from an Edgar Cayce reading for a woman who wanted to know why she hadn't been given an incarnation during the Palestine era in which her present son and husband had incarnated. She was told that she was there, but not in the flesh. She was, as some of us would term it today, a "guardian angel" for her present son while he lived and worked in that period.

A group of souls may find themselves together again and yet not one of them desired it to be so. In these cases, it is often the forces of the Universal Law that cause them to come together. For better or for worse they now have to meet the effects of their past actions with each other. The Universal intention is that the confrontation will lead to a resolution of their karma or at least a recognition of how their past actions with each other have caused the present predicament, and they will resolve not to act that way again.

Both in individual and group relationships, the karmic effects of past actions with others can create some very difficult, even terrible situations. The meeting can result in murder, rape, torture and other atrocities. Even in lesser cases karmic effect can result in back-biting, back-stabbing, bickering, fighting and other turmoils. Imagine what might happen if the universal forces of cause and effect brought together the souls of the Roman Coliseum and the souls they fed to the lions, or the Conquistadors and the Incas and Aztecs, or the Nazis and Jews.

The same cause-and-effect forces play a part in individual lives, too. Imagine if the Law brought together a victim killed in a family quarrel and his or her murderer. What about a soul who betrayed another's trust or love? What would be the reaction toward one another in this present Life? When lives are heavily burdened by the negative effects of their past actions, their present experience is often tragic, and occasionally their lives may appear to be wasted senselessly. However, from the soul's perspective a single incarnation is a learning-experience and an opportunity to resolve past actions that are now holding the soul back from a fuller life. One physical life is not the ultimate living experience for the soul. It is an opportunity to resolve the burdens past actions have placed upon our souls and to clear away the many ideas that continue to confuse and limit us. So even though the seventy or eighty years that comprise the average lifetime seem so very singular and final, it is only a temporary sojourn, a brief experience along an infinite path of soul-life.

Of course, all the good that has been experienced among the various souls and soul groups has just as strong an effect on present situations as does evil, and when we focus on this "good karma" we often find better ways to resolve the negative influences.

SOUL MATES

A "soul mate" is really nothing more than a soul or souls (and there may be several of them) with whom we have closely shared so many lifetimes that we now resonate to the same pitch, so to speak. We understand each other like no one else could hope to understand us. This acquired understanding gives soul mates the capacity to help each other in ways that would be difficult without the deep bonding that has occurred through the ages.

Soul mates often help each other reach their highest potential, and though this is not automatic and each will still have to apply themselves to making the present relationship the best it can be, their deep inner-knowing of each other gives them a distinct advantage. However, being soul mates doesn't automatically mean that they see eye-to-eye on everything. In fact, they are usually more like complements one to another than duplicates of each other, each one bringing to the relationship something the other is missing, thereby rounding-out the relationship and giving each of them more than they would have separately.

When soul mates are together, they form a dynamic bond and provide a source of strength for one another that is very hard to find in our world. They may presently be in either sex and interact with each other in any number of relationships. There is a strong tendency to think of soul mates only in the sense of lovers and marriage mates, but they can also be partners, parents, siblings, teammates, friends, etc. Having been lovers and mates in many past lives, however, it would be very hard for them to avoid at least a romantic interlude in the present life – there would simply be too much magnetism for them to easily ignore each other and the physical attraction. If, on the other hand, they had been close friends or family members throughout their incarnations, they would be inclined toward a similar relationship in the present. The point is, a soul mate is not always a sexual mate.

Another important point about soul mates is that the true mate of every soul is its Original Companion, the Creator, who gave each soul life for the very purpose of being eternal companions with Him. As far as the sexual dynamics of soul mating, it's important to keep in mind that in the heavenly home we (our souls) "neither marry nor are given in marriage." As souls, we are actually siblings in the Universal Family. Therefore, even though soul mates may give each other the support that is needed and deserved in this difficult world – which may include healthy, intimate, sexual companionship – they are ultimately brothers and sisters in the spiritual realms.

TWIN SOULS

This brings us to one of the strangest concepts concerning soul relationships, that of "Twin Souls." As we have already seen, a soul possesses both the male and female forces within itself prior to entering the duality of the Earth. As the soul enters the world it usually selects one of its two sexual natures and projects the unique characteristics of this sex while incarnate. As difficult as it may be to understand, the unmanifested sexual part of our soul can actually incarnate at the same time we do. In other words, our soul, which is much more complex than we have imagined, is capable of separating its dual sexual nature into two separate and distinct entities, one male and the other female, and each of these two entities can incarnate into the Earth at the same time in separate bodies that usually complement the present sex. That is to say that somewhere out there in the physical world is literally our other half – the other sexual aspect of our soul!

Fortunately, there are some examples of this in the Cayce readings. One of the more notable is a group of four souls who, in their present incarnation, were husband, wife, eldest son and a female business associate who was also a very close friend of the family. The husband was told through Cayce readings that his present wife was his soul-mate and that his life would never have reached its fullest potential without her. However, it went on to say that the female business associate and close friend of the family was his "twin soul"; in other words, she was the other sexual half of his complete soul. Furthermore, his wife's twin soul was their eldest son! I realize how bizarre all of this sounds, but the dynamics and dimensions of life are simply far greater than we imagine.

Of course, not all examples are as closely knit as this example from the Cayce readings. Generally, the twin soul relationship is presently found among spouses, friends, occasionally as parent and child, and sometimes the twin soul isn't even incarnate at the same time. However, there does seem to be a pattern that most twin soul relationships follow. In their early incarnations together they tend to be mates or at least seek a lover's relationship with each other, while in later incarnations with each other they tend to seek less sexually involved relationships and more work-related activities together, especially when the work has a soul purpose. This could be due to the involution/evolution process where, in the early periods of the descent into materiality they tended to continue their self-seeking, self-satisfying pursuits; but on the ascent toward a return to spirituality they tended to seek more holistic purposes and relationships. That is not to say that all present sexual relationships are self-seeking. From the Cayce material we find healthy support for marriage and home, and all the natural sexual aspects that are a part of the union of two in love and mutual caring.

PARENTS & CHILDREN

As difficult as it may be for us to believe, each soul actually chooses its parents – with one exception. If a soul has abused its gift of free will, then it comes under the strong influence of the Universal Law and is carried along on the force of its past actions into present relationships that it simply must face up to. Of course, no soul is given more than it can handle, not that it won't suffer, but it won't be totally lost or destroyed by the burdens of its karma. Generally, however, a soul chooses its parents prior to entering the Earth.

As we would expect, souls who have had experiences together in past lives will have a stronger attraction for each other than souls who have had no past experiences together. Even if souls aren't particularly fond of each other they still tend to be drawn together by the force of their past interaction. Furthermore, if the soul has a specific purpose for incarnating, and most of us do, then it will be seeking others who are a part of fulfilling its purpose or those who can at least contribute to it. Again, this doesn't mean that the childhood family life will be all hugs and kisses. In every relationship one can find advantages and disadvantages, and in order to enjoy the advantages one must accept the disadvantages. In fact, in many cases, the disadvantages lead to or create the opportunities for the advantages. When a soul is trying to decide which channels (parents) would be best for it to enter this world, it has to accept the limitations of this particular family as well as the opportunities.

From the spiritual realm Earth-life appears much like a river when viewed from high above, a bird's eye view. The soul who is deciding which channels to enter through sees the river in all its vastness, with many tributaries and branches, and it sees where the parents' boat is on this river of life. In this way it has an overview of what life will be like with these parents. However, because the river of life has many side-routes, the incoming soul can only see the strongest current in the parents' lives. It can't be sure that one of the free-willed parents won't change its mind and begin pursuing a different course, or that the currents themselves won't change course and thereby change the family's future. It can't even be certain that it won't change its own mind once it gets into the boat.

Destiny and fate do exist, and they exist side by side with free will. The effects of our past actions have an inertia that carries over into the present life and shapes it, thereby creating our destiny. However, nothing surpasses the power of the soul's divinely-given free will. At any time we can use our will to change directions, change attitudes, change purposes, change anything! In this way, our lives are both fatalistically foreshadowed by the cause-and-effect forces of our past use of free will, and yet amenable to change by our present use of free will. Therefore, the incoming soul can see only the general course of the family's riverboat; it can't be sure the family will stay the course.

The incarnate parents also have significant influence as to which soul enters through them. Their daily thoughts, desires and purposes create a beacon for souls who respond to these energies. This is particularly true of the mother. Her daily activities and inner thoughts during the gestation period create a field much like a magnet would, attracting souls to the field of opportunity life as her child would offer. As you would expect, more than one soul may be attracted to the same mother-to-be. In such cases, the forces of cause and effect, the will power and desire of the mother and the souls wanting to incarnate combine to make the selection. The souls who were not chosen for the present entry may well come in through a later pregnancy if the opportunity is presented, becoming siblings of the souls who entered first; or they may go on to other families with whom friendships or other blood relationships would naturally form and be maintained with the original channel family.

The soul generally enters the baby body at or near the time of birth. In one unusual case in the Cayce readings, the soul did not enter for two days after the birth of the baby. When asked about the delay, Cayce responded that the soul was all too aware how very difficult life would be should it choose to enter, and it wasn't at all sure it wanted to go through with it! Cayce was then asked what kept the baby's body alive for two days while the soul wrestled with its decision, and he responded, "the spirit." For Cayce, the soul was the entity, with all its personal memories and aspirations, and the spirit was the life force.

According to the metaphysical work of Rudolf Steiner, the soul actually incarnates in four stages. 1) A first level of consciousness enters at or near the time of birth. 2) A second and greater level of consciousness enters around the time the child cuts it first teeth. 3) A third level enters during puberty. And, 4) The final and complete entry of the soul occurs close to the age of twenty-one.

Most sources agree that the first couple of years of life are primarily devoted to developing the physical body and that the years from two to seven shape much of the child's sense of self and its view of the world. In addition to the well-known physical and emotional changes that occur during the course of puberty, Cayce and other metaphysical sources add that this is the time when karmic influences begin to take hold, coinciding with the release of hormones. This perspective sheds so much light on the otherwise baffling or incomprehensible changes in personality and behavior that sometimes accompany this stage of physical development. Around the age of 21 the individual begins to assume its major course through life. From here on the life progresses through a series of experiences and decision crossroads. These occur in natural and identifiable cycles, the most influential being the Seven Year Cycle: 1-7, 8-14, 15-21, 22-28, and so on. Notice how these cycles coincide with the general metaphysical cycles of: Birth; seven years of age; puberty (though puberty usually occurs before age 14, it is fulfilled at or near this age); and twenty-one years of age.

Furthermore, each soul experiences life in two primary arenas 1) The inner world of self, which includes one's mental and emotional being and physical body. 2) The outer arena of life's unique circumstances, including the social, economic, racial, national and religious environment, all of which are generally set at birth and the outer world has pre-structured in specific ways.

EXAMPLES

In order for us to really understand how all of this occurs in life and relates to our own lives, let's look at some real-life examples.

Like most young girls, Linda Mills wanted to fall in love with a wonderful man, have a family and live a rich, full life. When she met her future husband, she was genuinely attracted to him, though she knew he wasn't everything she had dreamed about. She especially didn't like his tendency to make decisions for her. Nevertheless, their love for each other was strong and they felt a deep mutual attraction. An added joy was that they were quite comfortable with each other around their friends and family.

They married and had two daughters. For Linda, the first daughter was a joy. Throughout the pregnancy and after the birth she and her new baby were very comfortable and happy with each other. They spent many wonderful hours together nursing and rocking while Linda softly hummed lullabies. But life with her second daughter was quite a different story. The pregnancy was uncomfortable, filled with sickness and stress, and after the birth she and the baby just never seemed to get into sync with each other. The baby didn't seem to enjoy being held or rocked like the first child and breastfeeding was a battle. In fact, the baby developed an allergy from the breast milk, and formula had to be substituted. Only the father's touch was comforting to this little one, and as she grew up her preference for him became even more evident. She was clearly "Daddy's little girl," while the first child was certainly Mommy's.

When this family received a past-life reading from Edgar Cayce, the cause of many of their present feelings and actions quickly surfaced. Apparently, Linda and her husband had been husband and wife before, but in the incarnation just prior to this one, they had been father and daughter, respectively. His tendency to make decisions for her and control her life was a carry over from being the father. In that past life Linda had been a rather wild and rebellious child. This was due in part to her resentment that the man who had been her equal in many lifetimes was now her father. It was a difficult life for him, too. Raising her was very hard, especially after the death of his wife in that lifetime. Naturally, all of these feelings carried over into their present life and marriage.

As for the children, the first daughter had been Linda's close friend through many lifetimes, bringing this love and friendship into the present life. In their most recent past life, the first daughter had helped Linda deal with the problems Linda had had with her father (Linda's present husband), and now as their daughter she would do so again. Now the second daughter had been the father's lover in many past lives, so you can just imagine the mutual enmity this created between the mother and daughter in the present. Linda's milk wasn't all the baby was allergic to! Neither did she want Linda's love and comfort as much as she did her father's. The father and his second daughter would have to learn to love each other in a much different way or break one of the strictest taboos, incest. All of these feelings were occurring subconsciously, of course, subtly affecting the conscious life.

As we can see, the deep currents of past experiences were playing a significant role in their present relationships. According to the Cayce readings, their goal now, from their souls' point of view, was to live together again and make an effort to accentuate the love and virtues, and minimize the resentments and bad habits they carried with them as a result of their past.

In another case, despite all his efforts to ignore or resist it, Michael Parks was afraid of the dark. His fear of the dark was not like most children's; he was deathly afraid, to the point of suffocating if left in the dark too long. As far as he and his parents could recall, his childhood was rather normal and nothing had occurred that might have caused this fear. Yet, during all of his childhood life in his parents' home, anyone in charge of him had to be aware of his fear and take precautions to insure that he was never inadvertently left alone in a dark room or house. His parents were very tolerant of his fear, caring for him in every way and were unusually understanding and sympathetic. And later, when he married and started a home and family of his own, his wife assumed the burden of his fear. She too proved to be very patient with him. Together they worked out an elaborate scheme whereby he could go to bed with the lights on and she would come to bed after he had fallen asleep. Only then would she turn the lights off so she could fall asleep. Even so, if he awoke during the night, he would become extremely anxious and uncomfortable. He would have to fight to keep himself from panicking before turning on his bedside light. But once the light was on, the only way he could get back to sleep was to go into the living room, turn on all the lights and sleep on the couch, knowing the lights would be on while he slept.

One night Michael awoke from a terrifying dream, a dream that was to be the beginning of his conquering the fear. He dreamt he was in a dark dungeon surrounded by wet stone walls that went up so high he couldn't see where they ended. There was absolutely no way out and no one was coming to help him. As he stood there he began to cry. He cried so long and hard that the cell began to fill with his tears. When he noticed the tear-water was up to his chest, he tried to stop crying but couldn't get hold of himself – it all seemed too horribly fixed, so unchangeable that he felt completely trapped without hope of ever seeing light or life again. Eventually, the pool of tears reached his nose and he had to stand on his tiptoes to breathe, yet he continued to cry. Slowly he allowed himself to ease under the water, drifting into a sorrowful, lonely dream of letting go, surrendering his will to the reality of his predicament. At this point he awoke from the dream. The sheets were soaked and his body was covered with chilly sweat. When he told his wife and parents the dream they cried and were very upset by it. However, underneath, Michael was beginning to feel pretty good. In fact, he noticed his fear of the dark had actually diminished since the dream. It was as though something in that dream had healed and changed him.

About a year later Michael happened to take part in a series of exercises for recalling past-life experiences. From the information he received during these exercises and several more dreams over the next two years, he began to understand why he was afraid of the dark.

In a previous incarnation he had been a renegade from the courts and causes of Louis XIV. So violent and disruptive were his counter-attacks against the king that he became one of the most wanted men in France. His raids destroyed many of the king's storehouses, and his ability to elude capture created a great deal of hatred among the king's soldiers charged with capturing him. One day they did capture him and in retaliation for his actions and also as a result of their frustration with trying to stop him, they threw him into the bottom of a well-like dungeon, covered it and left him there to die a slow death. In this terrible place of complete darkness, he managed to survive for several days. In the beginning he was sure his friends and his wife would come to his rescue. But as time went by he realized that no one was coming and he lost hope and died. In the latter days of his ordeal he lost all sense of time and his mind began to fall apart. He could no longer be sure of what was real and what was illusion. But the worst part was the unrelenting darkness and confinement. This was what his soul remembered and most feared.

Just as we might expect, his current parents and wife, who helped him deal with his fear in the present life, had been the very people he had counted on to rescue him from the dungeon. His father and his wife had been his close friends and colleagues-in-arms, while his present mother had been his wife in the French incarnation. They didn't go to his rescue because he had become so notorious that it would have been too risky to attempt to save him without being captured and thrown into the dungeon with him. To a great degree, his own actions had brought him to this end, yet his parents and wife regretted that they had not at least tried to rescue him. His present-life dream was too much for his parents and wife to hear without deeply reacting to his ordeal. However, Michael's reliving the experience in his dream somehow released him from his life-long fear of the dark.

In yet another less dramatic case, a man who had fallen in love with a divorcee found himself struggling with his feelings. He eventually married her and tried to be the best stepfather to her child he possibly could, but when he discovered that he could not father children himself, he felt cheated and fought feelings of resentment toward the special relationship between his wife and her child. When he received a past-life reading from Edgar Cayce, he was told that in a previous incarnation in ancient Greece he had been married to the same woman. In that life she was the one unable to conceive a child. Though aware of her sadness and heightened sensitivity because of the added implications of being barren in those days, he chose a second wife to bear him a child. He further shamed and humiliated her by bringing the second wife and child to live in the same house, forcing her to witness the open joy and affection expressed in the little family. In his present-life circumstances, according to Cayce, he was merely meeting himself: though he deeply desired his own offspring, he was impotent; and though living in his own home, he felt like an outsider to the love shared within it.

Taking advantage of the present situation and making life as miserable as possible for her husband would simply be setting herself up for a future destiny of sadness. The law of karma is very impersonal: What one does, one experiences, without exception. If this woman now chose to help her husband meet his fate as best she could, she would heal many wounds and free herself at the same time.

In still another case, a beautiful woman from the modern cosmopolitan life of a big city came to Cayce and described her tragic predicament, asking for a remedy. Her present husband was impotent and she was a beautiful woman in the prime of her life. Why? Why was she in such a tragic situation? she lamented. She went on to say that there was another man she knew at work, and she wondered if she could have an affair with him yet remain with her husband...because she did love her husband; she simply wanted to fulfill all of her womanhood. Cayce responded by showing her why she was faced with such a dilemma.

In a past incarnation during the Crusades, she and her present husband were also married to each other. He was then one of the greatest of the Crusaders, often going off to war. However, every time he left, he saw to it that she wore a chastity belt, literally putting her under lock and key! Then and there she swore deep in her heart she would get even with him, and now, Cayce said, she had him right where she'd always wanted him – in a position where she could make him pay dearly.

What a triangle! I wouldn't be surprised if the other man had also been hanging around the castle while the rest of the men were off to war. At any rate, here they were again, set up perfectly to play out resolution or revenge for past actions with each other. The husband had used his free will to squash his wife's, forcing her to submit to his sexual restraints without any choice on her part. Now he found himself sexually restricted and frustrated, and completely subject to her will and her choices. She now had the power to make him pay.

But this was a loving as well as lovely woman. She found herself torn by her marriage vow and her desire to simply enjoy her physical beauty and youth. Paradoxically, she also found herself wanting to make a success of her marriage and her home, and despite his past wrong, she loved her husband and he returned that love in so many ways. If only he were able to sexually fulfill her. What a tangled web. The choice was completely hers; nothing was standing in her way.

Cayce advised her to do whatever she would want done to her if she were in her husband's shoes, and she did. She withdrew from the other man's affections and built a loving home with her husband. We might well feel that she suffered twice in the relationship, but if she had only not wanted revenge on him, she wouldn't have had to be with him again. true karma was within him. She got involved aga[in?] her desire to get even with him. No doubt she [will] eventually incarnate into a life filled with physical, mental, emotional and spiritual happiness and the rest of the world will probably look at her and think she is lucky rather than deserving.

One example of how past lives can affect non-family relationships is that of a businessman who happened to receive many readings from Edgar Cayce. In fact, these readings are just phenomenal in what they reveal "behind the scenes," so to speak, in illustrating what profound effects past-life experiences and emotions have on present relationships, and a "typical" business meeting, in this case.

When Walter Morrison walked into a board meeting, he was walking into a history that reached far beyond his present life. Amid the members of this board were souls who had been his conquerors, his servants, his concubines, his cohorts and his bitter enemies! Imagine what the underlying motivations were when Walter made a proposal which the group had to vote on, or when Walter had to cast his vote concerning a proposal by one of the other members of this band of souls. Who among the group would tend to support him? Who would tend to thwart his efforts and ideas? And who would he tend to support and resist? Many of these answers are predictable based on their past-life experiences with each other, experiences that they would innately respond to on a soul level because of their past affinities and antipathies for one another.

Walter himself was curiously amazed at how well the past-life readings predicted his present feelings for various members of the board. Only in a few cases did he find he really didn't have any particular innate reaction to a member. And in most cases, the members that consistently rubbed him the wrong way were those who had been on his bad side in past lives, and those that seemed to agree and support him consistently were those who had done so in the past.

When relationships are viewed with a past-life perspective, the dynamics of the behavior, including the attitudes and emotions in a relationship, become more than just current moodiness or general personality traits. There are undercurrents of memory that simply cannot easily be ignored. Before we look into how we can discover our past lives, let's look in the next chapter at another example from the Cayce material, an example that gives us an overview of soul-life and soul-history over many lifetimes.

8. DESTINY, FATE & KARMA

In order to fully appreciate the secret teachings, we need to understand how the Universal Law of Cause and Effect works. It's easy to say that the experiences in one's life are the result of past activities, but the forces of this law are greater than we may first imagine.

Every action, every thought, every idle word sets up reactions, according to the Universal Law. When one thinks a thought, that thought makes an impression on the Universal Consciousness. Nothing is lost or done in secret. Everything is done within the Universal Consciousness, and the Whole is affected by it (as well as all others within the Whole).

This isn't easy for us to believe, living in our own little worlds. Secret, private, alone and separate are active words in our vocabulary. This is due to our current separation in consciousness from the Whole. In the higher realms of consciousness there is no space. Things and people are not separate, but part of a Whole. All is actually One. All is within the Whole. By increasing the focus on self, we have created the illusion of a self separated from the rest of life, but it just isn't so. Our individual actions and thoughts make an impact on the Mind of the Universal One.

When the legendary seer, Edgar Cayce, was in the deeper levels of consciousness and was asked to give a "reading" of the soul-record for an individual, he found it very difficult to determine whether the soul had thought of doing something or had actually done it. In the deeper levels of consciousness, thoughts and actions are equal in their impact. Perhaps this explains Jesus' admonition that adultery in one's heart is the same as committing it in deed.

Thoughts are things. Thoughts are real.

Reactions to past thoughts and actions become our fate, destiny and karma. An individual's fate is simply the rebounding effects of previous choices remembered by its soul. The reason the effects of these previous choices often seem unfair to the conscious mind is because the personality doesn't see beyond its own life for sources of current conditions.

"Master, who did sin, this man, or his parents, that he was born blind?" (John 9:1-2) Now if these disciples didn't believe in and understand pre-existence of the soul and karma, why would they ask if this man's own sins had caused him to be born blind? The only way this could happen is for him to have sinned before his birth! And, in fact, that is just what they thought he might have done. Notice also how the disciples thought that his parents might have brought this upon themselves through past mistakes. Here is a clear indication that within the inner circle of Jesus' followers there was the concept that misfortune had a source, and that that source could extend beyond the present lifetime.

As companions of God, we are free to live and choose and grow almost as we desire, but not without being subject to Universal, Spiritual Law. Through meeting our thoughts, actions and words we learn to discern wisdom from folly, lasting strength from weakness and true life from illusion. In turn we become more able to fulfill our ultimate purpose for existing: to be a companion to the Universal Creator.

The law is actually a magnificent tool for perfect learning. It is completely impersonal – everyone experiences it equally and for the purpose of enlightenment, even Jesus: "Though he were a Son, yet learned he obedience by the things which he suffered." (Hebrews 5:8)

THE MEMORY COMPLEX

The law of karma is not some fierce god in the sky keeping track of everything so that it can zap people when they least expect it. Most karmic reactions in fact come from the individual's own deep memory of what it has done.

You see, actions and thoughts build a consciousness much in the same way that exercise and food build a body. In a way, we are a memory complex. Our body and mind is the sum total of all we have done. The memories, whether conscious or unconscious, make up our present condition. Thus, when we look at one another we are actually seeing a memory complex. Decisions are based on our past; reactions are based on our past; so are our goals. To understand a person, we must know something about their memory complex.

Not surprisingly, karma has been described as memory. Karma is memory coming to consciousness again. What has occurred in the past is recalled and has an effect on the present. Now, the recollection may not surface to the conscious level; the personality may have no awareness of the memory, in fact. Yet, it exists at the deeper, soul level. Nevertheless, the soul sees through the same eyes as the personality, and is reminded of its past use of free-will and consciousness. Naturally, some of these memories will be compatible with the Universal, and some will not.

Memory is an important concept in understanding how the law of karma works.

As a soul draws closer to the Universal Mind it becomes aware that some of its memories are not compatible with the Creator, and since its ultimate purpose for being is companionship with the Creator, it seeks out opportunities to resolve these incompatible memories.

Suppose a soul criticizes another soul among its peers and behind its back. As it becomes more aware of its true nature it will recall this wrong, and because of its incompatibility with the Creator, will seek to correct it. Now, the resolution could take many forms. The soul might seek out an opportunity to work closely with the injured soul as a supporter, assistant, publicist, agent or the like. Or perhaps it would seek to re-create the original scene – putting itself in a position to criticize the other soul again in front of the same peers. The test would be to see if the soul would choose not to criticize this time, even if it meant a certain loss of position for itself. Throughout all of this the soul grows wiser and more compatible with the Creator.

If, however, a soul has gotten so far away from its true nature that it has no conscience, then the Law can become a formidable obstacle to any further free-will action. Such a soul becomes surrounded by its karma; everywhere it turns it meets the terrible effects of its previous actions and thoughts. Yet, even a soul who has gotten in this pathetic situation can return to perfection because there is no total condemnation from the Creator or the Law. If the soul turns away from its self-centeredness and begins acting, reacting, thinking and speaking like a companion to the Universe, then the Law is just as perfect as it is with error; and the reactions begin to build and establish a new destiny for that soul.

Karma is memory. As one recalls or relives situations, one meets self again, and a new decision point or crossroads is presented to the soul. "Before thee are set good and evil. Choose thou." (Deuteronomy 30:15) In our portrait of life, good would be equated with compatible, harmonious actions and thoughts which consider the needs and desires of others along with self's needs and desires; and evil with actions and thoughts that are motivated by a self-orientation that pays little or no attention to the needs and desires of others and the Whole. Metaphysically speaking, good results in oneness, and evil results in a sense of separation. Decisions in one's life could be approached by evaluating which choices promote greater oneness and which promote separation.

However, it gets a little difficult to support this idea much further than that because in most of the secret teachings there is the belief that one must separate oneself from the world if one is to awaken to the greater reality beyond this life. Yet if we look closely at this belief, we find that the separation is more accurately a detachment than a separation. One is to strive to release oneself from the possessive power of the things of this world while still actively participating in it. In other words, one is to enjoy food and drink without being possessed by food and drink; one is to enjoy material life without being possessed by it.

Look at the "Seven Deadly Sins" of Western religion. Each of them (lust, envy, greed, gluttony, etc.) expresses a type of possessive power that overtakes the partaker. The "Seven Virtues" on the other hand, express selflessness on the part of the recipient: kindness, gentleness, patience, etc.

Notice also that the Sins are mostly self-experienced, but the Virtues require another person in order for them to be realized. This follows Jesus' teaching, "I seek mercy, and not sacrifice. He who has ears..." Sacrifice can be done alone, but mercy requires that one reach out beyond oneself and consider others and their needs.

Again, we come to the inevitable conclusion that sin is self to the exclusion of others and the Whole, while virtue is oneness with the Whole and consideration of others. It's important to note here that the ultimate goal is not the complete lose of self-identity, rather, as Cayce so aptly phrased it: to know yourself to be yourself, yet one with the Whole.

GRACE, MERCY AND FORGIVENESS

In one sense it is true that "not one jot or tittle shall be removed from the Law." One must meet every bit of its karma. However, there is a way that it can be modified, softened, even ameliorated. If a soul, knowing another soul has wronged it, forgives that soul and holds no lingering resentment – perhaps has even forgotten the wrong in the depths of its forgiveness and understanding – then it begins to take hold of the power of forgiveness. The more it forgives, the more it perceives and understands forgiveness. Then, when it approaches the Universal Consciousness and realizes it possesses memories that are incompatible with the It, forgiveness is much more viable, removing the barrier between Father/Mother and son/daughter. The law is so precise (what one gives one receives; no exceptions) that if one begins having mercy on and forgiveness of others, one begins to receive mercy and forgiveness upon oneself. Now, the law is very sensitive to the deep, true purpose for which one does something, and if the purpose for forgiving another is simply to obtain forgiveness for oneself, then little is gained. But if one truly forgives, and forgives by understanding, through empathy and compassion, then there is no way one can avoid receiving forgiveness upon oneself. Unless, of course, one refuses to forgive oneself. Here the law is held captive to the absolute power of free will given each soul.

The law also works in some very curious ways. Somehow one's greatest weakness possesses the potential to become one's greatest strength. With each difficult situation, whether physical, mental or spiritual, there comes an opportunity. These "opportunities" sometimes appear to be hopeless problems, like a crippling disease, an uncontrollable habit or a situation in which one feels totally victimized without cause. More often they appear as annoyances or frustrations, like an unattractive nose, a difficult sibling, spouse, colleague, boss, lover or friend; or an ever present lack of money. In each case, the soul has an opportunity to resolve and overcome some weakness in itself, and by doing so with the right attitude, the soul can rise to new heights of consciousness, love, and companionship. Attempting to sidestep one's crosses is simply a temporary diversion, delaying the eventual glorification that is the soul's inheritance when it is sought.

All has to be met. And yet, no soul is given more than it can bear to carry – this is the paradoxical blessing hidden in the limitations of time and space. A soul is given the time it needs to turn away from its selfish ways and, like the prodigal son, return home to a feast of joy and welcome from its Father in heaven. Reincarnation is not a way to avoid judgment and responsibility;, it is a way to allow the soul enough time to correct its mistakes and develop itself.

FATALISM & FREE WILL

How can free will coexist with fate?

Suppose while traveling on a road you arrive at a point where the road divides into two and you must decide which road you will take. Once you make your decision, you have set a direction that can be almost totally predicted. In this way your fate is decided; but remember, it was your free decision that cast it in the first place. Now suppose that you could fly up in the air and get a bird's eye view of the road you selected to travel. From this vantage point you would see your future. The catch is that you couldn't be absolutely sure you'd stay on this road once you started. You might decide to go back to the beginning and take the other road, or you might choose to take a sideroad off of this road. You might even decide to sit down for a long time in one place along the road. In this way, your fate is before you, but you still have the free will to change your direction. It may take you some time before you can make a significant change, and perhaps it will require some considerable effort. For example, let's suppose you did decide to travel a different road. Where you are on the present road will in some way determine what options are available to you. There may be only one side-road within miles. You might be close enough to the beginning of the road to turn around, or too far down the road for that, in which case you'd have to push on until you could choose another route. Many of the decisions in our lives are like this. They are affected by our original choices, which may be long forgotten by now. The present road we're taking also affects our options. Nevertheless, no matter where we are in our lives, no matter what circumstances in which we find ourselves, once we finally wake up and take notice of what we're doing, our free will is at our disposal to effect the necessary changes. The only limitations are how long it will take us to get to the place where we can make a significant new choice, and how much effort will be required to get there.

"IT'S MY KARMA"

One of the most distorted views of karma is the idea that nothing can be done about it. No matter how terrible our predicament, there is always something we can do, even if it's just dealing with it as best we can with a patient smile, a good attitude and a loving heart. The time will come when we will be through with this stretch of the hard road, and it's best to come out of it with no bitterness. Remember, no one has done this to you, it is a result of your own actions, thoughts or words. In patience you will overcome it and rise again to an even greater level than before. Again, keep in mind that in the worst situation often lies the greatest opportunity.

THE CENTER IN THE MIDST OF CONDITIONS

From the ancient Taoist text, The Secret of the Golden Flower, we find another wonderful concept: Amid all the circumstances of our life, all its activities, all its demands, there lies deep within us an undisturbed, unmoved place of ultimate quiet and peace. This is the center in the midst of conditions. When we learn how to enter this place for short periods each day, the demands of the day lose much of their sting. We find we can not only cope better, but we can actually make better decisions and effect better use of our time and energy each day. Later, in the section on Meditation we'll look at some of the techniques for entering this special place.

Reincarnation & Karma

9. PAST-LIFE MEMORY

The question crying out for an answer is, "If we have lived before, why don't we remember it?" The answer is both simple and complex.

The simple answer is "Because we have not lived before."

This is not completely true, but it is relatively true because the "you" and "I" that we consider to be ourselves has not lived before. We think of ourselves as composed of personality (which includes the conscious mind) and body. The current conscious mind, personality and body are new; they have not been alive before. Nor have they reincarnated in the true sense of the word. However, our souls have been alive before – this is the distinction – and they have reincarnated. The memories are thus our souls', not ours.

Now, we might well ask, "If the memories aren't ours, how can they affect us?" It happens much in the same way that a father's memories affect his son. The son does not possess the father's memories but he'll not easily avoid the influence of those memories on his own life. If the son wishes to know of the experiences that shaped his father's attitudes, emotions, opinions, beliefs and personality, and subsequently affected the son, then the son must seek out the father and discover what life has been like for him.

In a similar way, our souls' memories are not consciously our own, but since we are the offspring of our souls, we can't help but be influenced by them. If we are to understand these influences, we must seek out our souls and learn of their experiences. Only then can we completely understand why we are the way we are, and consequently why our lives are the way they are.

Now that I've given the simple answer, let's look at the more complex aspects of past-life memory.

Upon death, the mind and soul are released from the body. Depending upon the individual's level of consciousness, he or she will either perceive this transition or, in ignorance, become bewildered and confused by death.

No longer will communication with friends and relatives who remain incarnate be possible, for the soul can no longer vibrate the vocal cords of the now dead body, producing sounds that vibrate the ear drums of the incarnate. Nor can it any longer animate the dead body, reflecting Earth-light off its surface so that it can be seen by carnal eyes. The new, non-physical "body" does not project into the third dimension, so it can't be seen by three-dimensional beings. Usually, it is this initial inability to communicate and be seen by humans that causes the soul to realize that "death" has occurred. When this realization reaches its ultimate enlightenment, the conscious mind begins to relinquish its hold on consciousness, much in the same way consciousness is relinquished when falling asleep. Thereafter, the subconscious mind rises to become the more dominant consciousness, as it does during sleep. Eventually, the subconscious mind, which is a higher-dimensional mind, will become the operative consciousness for life beyond the three dimensions of Earth.

In order to reincarnate and function in Earth's dimension, the soul must develop another three-dimensional consciousness. Since this new conscious mind is neither the consciousness used in the realms beyond physical life nor the conscious mind used in the former incarnation, it does not possess of itself any memories of previous lives. Such memories are stored deep within the subconscious, the soul's mind.

At or near the time of death, the strongest influence during the most recent incarnation will become prominent, much in the same way that the strongest influences of an Earth day affect the dreams of night. This influence will act as an impelling force upon the soul. As the soul takes stock of the life, it will be moved by this force and seek or be driven toward its next environment – ever reaching for or being forced to accept that environment it has earned.

How all of this occurs depends on the level of spiritual awareness possessed by the dying individual. In cases where there is little or no awareness, the forces of direction are involuntary, ruled by the Law of Cause and Effect. However, where there is some awareness of spiritual purpose and reality, the soul can use its free-will during this transition to move toward a dimension of life of its own choosing.

In whatever environ it seeks or finds itself, the soul may sojourn for only a few Earth-years or for many thousands before it returns to Earth. In the Cayce readings there are many examples of souls varying the length of time away from Earth.

An example of a short period between incarnations is that of a little girl who was killed during the bombing of England in World War II. She reincarnated within a year of her death. Because she had an uncontrollable fear of loud noises, her mother came to Edgar Cayce for help. The reading revealed that the child's soul had not completely withdrawn from the Earth's environs after that life, causing memories of the bombings to be very near the surface consciousness. Consequently, during loud noises, her subconscious would bring forth images, smells and sounds, causing her to actually reexperience the bombings with all the emotions of the original moment. She would relive the separation from the mother, the confusion, and the accompanying anxiety. No amount of reassurance that these were just fantasies was going to help the child. They were not fantasies to her. She experienced these things. And sadly, as far as she was concerned, these terrible noises and their destruction were an integral part of Earth life.

Cayce's advice was: reassure the child that this is a new life, a new opportunity. (This approach would be as acceptable to her subconscious mind as telling her that these were unjustified fantasies would not.) And be sure, he advised protectively, that scary stories and the like are not introduced to her.

Cayce also gave readings which stated that many of the souls reincarnating toward the end of the 20th century and the beginning of the 21st, were ancient Atlantians who had not reincarnated since Atlantis! According to Cayce's own timetable, this would mean that these souls had not reincarnated for hundreds of thousands of years. The reason, according to Cayce, was that their technological understanding was so great that there simply wasn't anything on Earth to interest them until the industrial and technological revolutions began.

These souls would be experiencing their new Earth-life much differently than the little girl from

World War II. Afterall, they would have had over one hundred thousand years to assimilate and temper the effects of their most recent incarnation. Those souls who had been reincarnating more frequently might perceive these returning Atlantians as rather awkward people. According to Cayce, they would not have as natural an understanding of Earth-life as souls who had been reincarnating frequently. They might not know, for example, to come in out of the rain, or to tie their shoes to avoid tripping, or appreciate the cycles of night and day, awake and asleep. They might not have as much understanding of their bodies as we do. In many ways they would be strange, and the Earth would be strange to them. On the other hand, they would likely have an unusually high understanding of the forces of the Cosmos, such as electricity, physics, relativity, etc.

If past-life memories abide in the mind of the soul, it would seem that all one has to do is to get in touch with one's soul and the memories will pour forth. Alas, it's not that easy.

As best as I can determine from years of study, observation, and personal searching, our souls' reality is quite different from our conscious, three-dimensional reality. In the realm of the soul there is no time, no space. Try as we might, it is hard for us to understand a realm in which linear perception of time does not exist; where spacial separation isn't known. In other words, there is no past, no future; no here and no there. The soul apparently perceives life as a whole. Thus, here and there are the same; yesterday and today are one. Because of this, the memories of past lives are not laid out on an easy-to-read linear timetable for us to scan and comprehend. This is not to say that they can't be translated into linear terms so that we can see with our time/space consciousness, but that requires a skill few acquire.

Let me explain this as I have come to understand it. There is evidence that the deeper consciousness stores memories in clusters rather than in sequence. These clusters have little relation to the time frame in which they occurred; in other words, they are not identified by time but rather by similarity. For example, memories of grief are clustered together, and are not easily separated into a timetable based on when our souls experienced the grief. Therefore, when one attempts to go into the soul's mind and retrieve memories, one may come upon the "grief cluster" and get a collection of scenes from many different occasions related to grief.

I just used the description "scenes related to grief," but when a person actually contacts their grief cluster, it is much more emotional than this description conveys. I've observed individuals recalling, or more properly, reliving, experiences of their souls. I can tell you that even though we don't have a conscious awareness of these memories, they are very, very much a part of us. And when we do contact them, we can expect to be amazed at how powerful they are and how familiar. A natural result of such contact is a catharsis. Often, the outer individual will later say, "I always 'knew' this but could never express it."

The veil between our conscious and our unconscious is so fine that the slightest turn in the mind can make direct contact. And yet, it is so perpendicular to our current world, that no amount of conscious effort can make it happen. Nevertheless, when we make contact, despite our present assurances that we have no memory of another part of us and its experiences, we will come to realize that we knew even when we said we didn't. It's that subtle, that close.

I observed a woman coming into contact with her grief cluster through a technique called Guided Imagery Music (GIM). I thank God that this occurred in the presence of an experienced, well-trained, clinical therapist. (The therapist was Carol Bush, author of the book, Imagery and Music: Pathways to the Inner Self available through Inner Vision.) The power of this patient's grief was more than I could have dealt with myself. Her body writhed when it contacted the grief; the room filling with her soul's sorrow and pain. A powerful, emotional force rose out of her unconscious to a level greater than I had ever witnessed. However, after several therapy sessions, she was a new woman! Happy, hopeful and somehow released from the grief that had possessed her soul.

As for this woman's past-lives, the GIM method revealed seemingly disconnected scenes of terrible destruction and death. The images that came forth were of towns and roadsides after what seemed to have been battles or wars. After these battles, the women who survived had to live among the dead, struggling to rebuild their lives with nothing. Bodies were everywhere; mostly, she recalled, children's bodies. Sometimes the scenes she described were so sorrowful, so pitiful that I couldn't bare to hear any more. Yet, today I look around the world and see women in similar scenes of terrible destruction and death – Lebanon, Ethiopia, Cambodia, Armenia, and on and on. At some point, these women will also need to be healed of their grief, as this woman was.

In addition to this clustering characteristic, soul memories often reflect their presence through recurring situations and patterns of behavior in our lives, and are in fact, the surface-signs of subtle soul-memory in action. All of us have noticed ourselves or others struggle with recurring tendencies to attract certain situations or people in our lives. "He was always attracted to losers." Or, "She never could handle disappointments." "He never believed he was good enough, or smart enough, or rich enough, etc."

If we find ourselves experiencing a certain situation or behavior again and again, you can bet we are seeing the effects of past activities involving the same type of situation or behavior. And the best thing we can do about it is face it in this life and make it right. If we have a weakness for something, we must strengthen ourselves. If we have barriers in our lives, we must patiently but consistently surmount them.

Let me give you another example from the Cayce readings. Edgar Cayce himself had a strong tendency to sink into deep, dark depressions when things began to go wrong in his life – more than would be considered normal for any of us. When he received one of his own readings on this tendency, he was told that it was the result of an action he chose in a past life in ancient Troy. He had been one of the guards at the gates of Troy when the Greeks brought the gift of the towering horse. When the Trojans realized that they had been tricked, and subsequently lost their city and the war because of it, Cayce couldn't bear it and took his own life. As a result of this past decision, he has to fight to keep himself from taking a similar course whenever things go bad for him. The reading went on to say that with every disappointment in this life, he had the opportunity to set a course, a new way of dealing with failure – a way that required more strength and purpose than his previous choice. Not surprisingly, he learned this lesson well and became quite patient with disappointments and setbacks, learning to endure beyond them to future successes.

For our purposes here, we need to see that here was a recurring behavioral pattern in his life: Whenever things went wrong he fell apart. Now, those around him at the time probably said to one another, as we might have, "Why does he take it so hard?" "Can't he handle the heat?" They may even have thought of him as "immature." The truth was that deep in his unconscious lay a memory of a failure and his choice in dealing with that failure. Now the pattern was set. Every future failure would "remind" him of this great failure, and he would begin again to think of himself as worthless and not deserving of life and another chance.

Remember the woman with so much grief in my previous story on GIM? Her personality and life displayed patterns related to these past-life experiences. She had an unusually emotional sensitivity to children. She couldn't stand any form of violence, especially where children were concerned. Though she adored children and desired intensely to have her own, she was afraid to have them for fear of losing them. All patterns of behavior stemming from her soul's experience with death and war.

Other souls who have not had the experiences that Cayce and this woman had would in all probability not find these as patterns in their own lives. On the surface, they might not understand why Cayce and the woman react to life the way they do, or why situations have such an impact on them.

Recurring patterns of behavior are surface-signs of past-life experiences and decisions, as are recurring situations. Keep an eye open for them, for they are part of your soul's karma and need to be dealt with and healed. As some have described them, they are signs of "unfinished business."

TECHNIQUES FOR RECALLING PAST-LIFE MEMORIES

It is possible to get the soul's perspective translated into a time-space reality for our use. For Edgar Cayce, the time-space setting was a "book." His deeper self perceived another soul's story as written in the "book of life," and his soul traveled to a Hall of Records where the Book of Life of each soul was stored. When looking at a soul's record, he turned the pages of the book back to the left and perceived that he was moving through time into this soul's past; flipping pages to the right, he looked into their future. The book was a translating tool. However, when pressed on the issue, Cayce's deeper consciousness would respond to the question of time and space as not existing in the higher dimensions.

But, for our purposes, we need the translation into time/space reality. Some of the major techniques making contact with our past-life memories are: Hypnotic Age-Regression, Reverie, Guided Imagery, Bodywork, Psychic Readings, and Self-Realization. Self-Realization includes such things as deja vu, intuitive perception, spontaneous realization, dreams, visions and many other awakenings that arise from within the individual.

REGRESSION, REVERIE, GUIDED IMAGERY...

Regression, reverie, guided imagery and various forms of bodywork all begin by getting the conscious self into a passive, relaxed condition, allowing access to the deeper consciousness; or, some might say that it is allowing the deeper consciousness to rise closer to the surface. However we look at it, these techniques seek to subdue the normal outer self and access the inner self.

Reverie, guided imagery and bodywork don't set up a time-space reality as clearly as regression. In regression the outer self is given a time reality to work within. The subject begins going back along the time continuum of his or her current life until the time of birth. At this point the suggestion is given to continue beyond and describe scenes that occurred before birth. This is actually how some heretofore traditional psychotherapists stumbled unknowingly into the very real realm of past-life memory.

In reverie and guided imagery, the conscious self is simply encouraged to view images from the subconscious, anticipating that the subconscious will speak to issues of importance to this soul. Or the outer self can be guided to images related to a specific issue. Past-life memories are not the primary focus of reverie, imagery and bodywork, although "cluster" memories as they relate to present issues (specific relationships, phobias, emotional pain, etc.) are usually forthcoming..

Where imagination ends and true past-life recall begins is difficult to say. There is no sure way to know whether the past life is imagined or true. In hypnotic cases, we know that the subconscious is so amenable to suggestion that even the slightest variation in the tone of the hypnotist's voice can give away his or her inclination and thereby prejudice the subject's subconscious to respond in kind. In reveries and guided imagery sessions, the conscious mind is encouraged to imagine, making it very difficult to know when one is imagining or having genuine past-life recall.

After observing several sessions with Carol Bush, and experiencing a few of my own, there are some ways that one can tell when something genuine is happening. Carol taught me to watch for a change in the nature of the images being experienced by the subject. There is a noticeable difference between images caused by outer stimuli and those coming out of true contact with the unconscious. It's as though the subject, who for the first part of the session seems in control of their images, loses control. The images begin to drive the outer person rather than the other way around. One also begins to see an emotional edge to the images. The outer person becomes affected by the images that it sees, no longer able to observe them objectively. These are signs, according to Carol and many other researchers, that genuine areas of reality in the inner person have been contacted . Whether they are actual indications of a previous incarnation of the soul or simply indications that the soul pre-existed, though perhaps not incarnate, is very difficult to determine, and doesn't really matter. The images are true expression from the unconscious and have great value if for that fact alone.

I suggest the only way we can be sure they are past-life recall is to be as honest about our reactions to the recall experience as possible. If there is simply no identification with the scenario, perhaps it is of no significance. However, I would also suggest that one never completely discard it because as our life continues we may begin to see how this suggested past-life recall may well have been part of our soul's experience. It was common for people who received Cayce past-life readings to write years later that they only recently became aware of just how accurate their reading was.

Another way to protect ourselves from excessive or confusing fantasy is to select the hypnotist or guide with great care. If possible, read some of their cases; interview some of their former clients. We need to use common sense in choosing both the person and the procedure to which we are subjecting ourselves. Our outer selves seem to have a built-in barrier protecting us from the direct impact of our soul's past experiences, especially those that are harmful or so unpleasant as to ruin any chance of correcting those mistakes in the present. This should be kept in mind when attempting to discover our souls' past. Some of the memories are hidden for a very good reason. Bringing them to the surface by force could prove disastrous, crushing the outer person under a burden that even his or her own soul would not have sanctioned. The past does need to be investigated and awakened, but the outer ego-personalities involved in these investigations (e.g., hypnotists, guides and even the subjects) must not assume they know what's best. The inner-soul must be allowed to reveal its secrets in a manner that suits its purposes and timing.

Before leaving these techniques for past-life recall, let's briefly look at body-memory.

All is really one. The physical body may appear to have a distinctly separate reality from that of the soul's, but in truth, it is a manifestation of the soul, and therefore contains within it the soul's memories. If we create the right atmosphere and perform certain manipulations, the body can connect with these memory "pockets" and release them.

Many times in the Cayce readings people were given past-life or even soul-sensitive reasons for present bodily marks, scares and mannerisms. Just a few examples would include the eldest son of Edgar Cayce who was told in a reading that scare that appeared on his hand every time he lost his temper was the soul's memory of losing that thumb in an angry past-life fight during the Crusades. The raged remains within him and manifest itself whenever he begins to lose his temper again. In another reading, a woman was told that the marks on her body (from birth) were given to her by a high priest when she first manifested in a physical body as reminders of her spiritual lineage.

There was also the case of a new born baby who was jaundice and when the nurses put him under the special lights to heal the jaundice a tattoo of an anchor appeared, remove him from the lights and you couldn't see anything! Perhaps the memories are right under our skin.

Now there are various techniques for releasing body-memory. Most of the ones I've learned begin with relaxing the body and mind, carrying it away with music, smells, lights or other stimuli, then massaging or pressing the body. Usually the practitioners are looking for the telltale sign that gives away the location of a memory – emotion! When an emotional reaction to touching a certain place on the body occurs, the practitioner begins to "work" that area, as he does, the participant begins to experience feelings, images, smells or sounds. There may only be an emotional feeling, such as grief, joy, love, etc., without any clear storyline, or there may be a most detailed story accompanying the release. Usually the recall or release begins with fragments and as the sessions continue, the story and meaning develops.

DREAMS

Two other sources for past-life recall are dreams and self-realization. Unfortunately, these are two of the least appreciated methods used today. Our dreams and self-realizations have an added bonus in that they not only provide us with past-life information but they do so in a way that builds a closer relationship between our outer and inner selves, integrating the two separate parts of our being. Building this bridge between our two islands of consciousness is vital to eternal life.

However, dreams and self-realization are certainly more difficult and long-term methods for discovering our past lives and the past lives of those who share our lives. The eventual friendship that develops from this reintegration of our Conscious with our Subconscious, our body with our spirit, our personality with our soul is worth all the effort involved.

Sleep brings our consciousness to the door of the subconscious. In this way, dreams are the conscious mind's recollection of the subconscious' activities during the deepest phases of sleep. If the conscious level recalls the dream, records it, studies it, discerns a meaning and, finally, uses the knowledge in its life, then the levels of consciousness begin to reunite and life takes on new dimensions. Since the deeper levels are not confined to the dimension of time and space, the past, even the distant past, is not difficult to know. Here the soul's story can be found. The following dream is an example of how a past life can be discovered through dreams.

I woke up around two or three in the morning thinking someone had made a loud noise in my bedroom. As I looked around I saw that everything was quiet. Nothing had happened. Lying back on my pillow I began to recall what I had been dreaming just before waking. The strong smell of horses, leather and sweat was overwhelming. It was as though these things were right in my bedroom. In my mind's eye I saw the side of a horse and a portion of a leather saddle. I couldn't have been more than a few inches from them. My vision was strange, it was as though I were looking through a pipe, I only saw what was directly in front of me, no peripheral vision at all. Slowly I started to look down at what I suppose were my feet, I was wearing black boots which were covered with a dry film of dirt. The ground around my feet was dusty dirt with little patches of scrub grass. I stared at my boots and the dirt for a long time. I began to feel how sweaty my feet were inside these boots and I didn't like it. Suddenly I heard someone behind me. He was calling me, but he was calling me 'Lexington.' Somehow I knew this was my name in this place so I turned around to see who was calling. As I looked at the man I knew he was my brother, Tim. He didn't look like Tim but I knew it was he. He told me to come over where he was and get something to eat before we rode on. It was as though I was drugged. It was very hard to walk but I managed to move over toward him and some other men sitting around a campfire. Like a slow-motion camera, my eyes took in everything though I didn't know what was going on. As I sat down to eat I began to smell the fire and the food. I still could smell horses, leather and sweat strongly but the smoke of the fire was strong and somehow familiar. I looked over at Tim and wondered if he'd noticed that I wasn't really Lexington. But he just looked up at me and told me to hurry up and eat, it wasn't safe for us to linger around here too long. Since I couldn't see except for what was directly in front of me, I began to worry that I wouldn't be able to find the food and eat. Somehow my hands found the food and I slowly ate. Then suddenly I realized that this was a past life, that I had actually lived this life with my present brother Tim. During this realization I had the feeling my mother in that life was behind me and I turned to see her. She introduced me to some of her friends. I was afriad she was going to ask me to tell them my name but I didn't know it. However, she turned to her friends and said, 'This is my son, Lexington.' I was dumbfounded. I just looked at her, dressed in the clothes of an Early American settler, and wondered what this was all about. Then just as suddenly I saw a map of North America. A dark, bold line began to move across the map and I knew it was showing me where I had traveled during this life-time. When the line stopped moving I knew that was where I died and I became uncomfortable because the death experience began coming back to me. The scene was once again around the campfire with my brother and the other men. Tim looked up at me and I knew he loved me. He also knew what was about to happen and his heart was sad because he didn't want me to die. I heard a rustling noise in the bushes to my left side but since my vision could only see directly in front of me I couldn't see who was coming. I felt a powerful flow to my head and as I started to lose consciousness I looked over at Tim who was shooting his gun as fast as he could and yelling, 'No, No! Don't die Lex! Don't die!' Somehow I knew we'd be together again but it was over for now, nothing could be done to keep me alive. My face was lying in the dusty dirt and I just stayed there, looking at the dirt, feeling my breath move in and out of my nostrils. I felt sorry for Tim. I didn't want him to be left without me and I didn't want him to be so sad. Somehow I felt I had always been a burden to him. I was never tough enough or smart enough for this wild, untamed country. I thought to myself, 'I'll make this up to him. I'll make sure the next time we're together I stay with him through the entire life, never leaving him.' Then I heard a whirring sound in my ears and I knew I was leaving this life. It was this noise that woke me.

In the present life this dreamer had a younger brother called Tim, and he was very protective of him. The two of them went everywhere together. However, the man who dreamed this dream was getting married in a week and was planning to move away from his younger brother to live in his wife's hometown. But the dream affected to much and so he asked his younger brother to transfer to a college in his wife's hometown. Tim did just that and the two of them continue to be very close.

Most past life dreams aren't so complete and detailed, revealing only fragments of a past life. Usually the fragment is an image, smell or sound that has left a lasting impression on the soul's mind. For example, a college professor frequently awoke from a nightmare in which he was choking on sand. The dreams were so real that he would actually be choking when he awoke. This professor was a white man who specialized in Black Studies. He had always found Black Culture and History to be of great interest to him. One day he was listening to a lecture by Alex Haley in which Mr. Haley told of how Africans kidnapped by the slave traders, bound and left on the beaches waiting to board slave ships, would commit suicide by deliberately swallowing sand. The professor was stunned. He knew immediately what his dream was about. He was recalling the most powerful image in his mind as he had committed suicide on the beaches of Africa in a previous life. A traumatic death experience from a past life is often recalled because of the profound impression it leaves on the soul's mind. Such was the case with this professor, the image and sensation staying with him in the form of a recurring dream.

Again, the only way we can distinguish between a true life recall and an imagined one is to objectively see how well it fits with our present character and life. In the case of the professor, his present interests and career supported the dream and the subsequent realization that he had lived a past life as a black African man who had committed suicide by swallowing sand.

Here's another example. The dreamer had this dream three days before he was to marry. He had been feeling anxious about the marriage because his bride-to-be did not have the same enthusiasm for the marriage as he did. Here's the dream he received.

Dreamt I was dressed in old Spanish clothing and did not look as I do today. In the dream I had dark hair and a beard. I was standing in a long rowboat that was slowly heading to shore. Somehow I knew we were off the coast of what is now called St. Augustine, Florida, but then it was wilderness. As we moved slowly toward shore I looked back at the ship that brought us here. It was surprisingly small for crossing the Atlantic Ocean; all wood and ropes and canvas. On the deck I saw Mary (my wife in the present incarnation), but she didn't look anything like she does today. She had black hair, dark skin and dark eyes, but somehow I knew it was Mary. She holding a small baby in her arms. As I watched them a strange image appeared over her shoulder. It was difficult to get this image in focus, I had to strain to see it. But as I looked very closely and intently, it began to take shape, and to my astonishment, it was my face as it is today! It was me, not as I was in the dream but as I look now – looking over her should back at me! Suddenly I knew what the vision meant, I was about to die and I would not be able to care for Mary and the baby, but he, my future self, would care of them in another life. I continued to stare at his face as if to get absolute assurance that Mary, the baby and I would have another chance. Glancing back at Mary and my baby, I began feeling very sad that they would have to continue life in this rough land without me to help them. As I looked back at his face I kept holding fast to the idea that he would be able to care for them in the future, and give them much of the joy they were going to miss in this lifetime.

Then I turned away and looked at the shore line. It was heavily wooded and desolate. There was no sign of trouble. Then, without warning, the beach was filled with savages. They were wild, crazy people, yelling and screaming with a violent madness that was terrifying. I watch the whole thing develop with a deep sense of my unavoidable destiny. I felt a piercing pain in my chest, penetrating the life inside me. As I fell into the water, I turned again to the ship and saw my wife and child on the deck, motionless, with the future face looking back at me over her shoulders. There was no expression on their faces, and as I slowly sank in the water I continued staring at them with all the feelings of the tragedy of the situation and what she and the child were going to have to go through without me to help.

Little wonder that his bride-to-be was not as enthusiastic about marrying him; she'd been with him before and it wasn't anything to hang your hopes on! This dream helped this young man. Not only did it give him an insight into one of his previous lives and its effect in his present life, but it gave him a clear view of a major purpose in this present incarnation, one that he had longed for – the opportunity to care for these two souls for whom he felt so much unfulfilled obligation.

Dreams are an excellent way to get in touch with our soul's memories; especially since the dream is actually the soul sharing an experience with the current personality.

SELF-REALIZATION

I'm using the term self-realization as a catch-all for intuitive perceptions, deja vu, spontaneous revelation, repetitive mental images, "gut feelings" and all the other forms of personal insight into one's deeper memories. If we open up to the possibility of reincarnation, we will begin to see many hints of our soul's past. Our natural talents, our taste in food, clothing and stories, our innate characteristics, our primary interests all indicate our soul's past experiences. Here's an example.

A young man was working at a printing and mailing company as a zip code sorter. It's a very non-mechanical job, requiring that one simply sort the mail by zip code. One Friday afternoon two of the printing press operators quit their jobs, leaving the company in a terrible bind. The zip code sorter asked the manager if he could come in the next day and work with one of the remaining printers to learn how to operate the presses. This was a ridiculous request because printing required a great deal of technical training and a lengthly apprenticeship before someone could correctly operate a press. But because the circumstances were so unusual, the manager gave him permission to try. The young man quickly became one of the best printers the company had. He said that it was all very natural for him. The smell of the ink was so familiar to him that he felt good being around it. The machines were so quickly understood by him, that he felt he had operated them before. And the process of printing was easily grasped. He went on to become the supervisor and eventually the manager of the printing operation.

On a visit to Williamsburg, Virginia this young man happened to walk into the old colonial printer's shoppe that had been restored to its original condition. Without any warning, he began to feel very strange. The smell of the wood, the ink and the sounds of the wooden press came rushing at him with such intensity he had to leave the building. After sitting outside for several minutes, he got up and went back inside the restored print shoppe. Slowly he walked through it, somehow he knew he had worked there in Colonial America. He observed how the costumed tour guides dressed and what they said about different items in the shop, and a deep sense of life's true breadth came upon him. He was never quite the same again. He had gained a new sense of the continuity of Life, and gained it in a very personal way. It was no longer an intellectual concept for him; he knew it first-hand.

PSYCHIC READINGS

Now you would think that anyone who studied and learned so much from the psychic readings of Edgar Cayce would be a strong supporter of psychic readings for past-life memory. But I'm not. Psychic readings are perhaps the least reliable of any method of getting past-life memories. It has been my experience that you can get a past-life reading from three different psychic and you'll end up with different past-lives. Often they will overlap in time, making it very hard to accept that they are correct. The psychics will give several reasons for these inconsistencies, but the fact remains, psychics rarely give the same lives to the same soul. Something is wrong. I don't know what it is, but its led me to be very skeptical of psychic readings.

Edgar Cayce was one of a kind. Even he recommended that we seek within ourselves for the answers, and avoid outside sources. That's why I prefer techniques that use the soul to tell the soul's story. However, I do believe some people are sensitive enough to "read" the Akashic Records, giving us some helpful insights into our past and its effects on the present. But you'll have to judge the results with care and common sense.

I recommend you seek within yourself. In the long run it will yield more than memories.

10. THE POWER OF AN IDEAL

For us to become companions to our Creator some changes are needed; our present condition is not nearly adequate for companioning with the Universal One. But before we change, we need to have a concept of what a companion is in its perfection. What is the true nature of a companion to the Consciousness of the Universe?

Now, before we blow our minds on this awesome thought or go running off to live in caves, let's hold to the guideline that the way is achieved step by step, a little here and a little there, and begins with what we presently have at hand. Even though the goal seems far beyond us, it isn't. Within us and our present circumstances exist the necessary tools for this transformation. Remember, the caterpillar shows no outward signs of its potential to become a butterfly, and we are much greater than a caterpillar.

First, we need a concept of what a companion is in its perfection. We need an Ideal, a standard by which we can measure and guide our progress through this metamorphosis. And a metamorphosis it is. We are intending to completely change form, from terrestrial to celestial, from flesh to spirit, from man to god. Has anyone already achieved this? Is there someone we can look to as an example? If we accept that Jesus became one with the Father, transfigured and resurrected his body, then He may well be our best ideal.

When I first got into the secret teachings and decided to begin this transformation, I couldn't accept Jesus as an ideal. Religion, as I experienced it in my early years, destroyed Jesus as an ideal for me. I was subjected to teachers who were convinced that fear was the beginning of holiness, and sin was as natural to humans as eating! It took me a long time to get over my terrible bias against anything religious, including the name with which they "beat" me. Perhaps my soul was meeting something it had done to others in the past. Perhaps, in a previous life, I had used Jesus to "club" others into submission, and now I was experiencing the devastating effects of this approach. Whatever, I found it very difficult to accept as an ideal the Jesus which had been presented to me.

Since then I have come to know a very different Jesus – a loving, humble, meek and long-suffering Jesus, with a mystical side that I had not known before. It is this Jesus that I now believe the secret teachings are talking about. And it is this Jesus that I suggest we consider as an ideal for the transformation. I don't mean his life as Jesus alone, though this is obviously the primary one to consider. But the complete story of this great soul's experiences – in other words, his other incarnations and their place in his preparation for the final transformation. It is not within the scope of this book to present all of His lives; I'll leave that to others (see Appendix for such books) or some future book. Let's focus on using an ideal to aid our transformation.

The Cayce readings make a distinction between Jesus and Christ. Jesus was a human being, like you and me; a man who lived among others in a physical world. He was truly a man in every sense of the word, with weaknesses and strengths common to all. He needed to sleep, eat, love and be loved. However, this particular man cooperated with the Universal Forces and maintained attunement with the inner presence of God. As he said, he and the Father are one.

Christ, according to Cayce, is the Spirit within this man. Christ is the light, the wisdom, the eternal aspect within the outer man. Here we see again the combining of flesh and spirit, terrestrial and celestial, man and god. It is the way of things in this world. Christ is the Spirit; Jesus is the man.

Truly, truly, I say to you, unless one is born of water and the Spirit, he cannot enter the kingdom of God. That which is born of the flesh is flesh, and that which is born of the Spirit is spirit. (John 3:5-6)

Christ manifested through a human being like ourselves, Jesus of Nazareth; son of Mary and Joseph, brother of James, friend of Lazarus, teacher of Peter and the others. He dined with Zacchaeus, wept with Mary and the others over Lazarus' passing, and asked John to care for his mother as he was dying. The great deeds were not this man's, but the Spirit within him. The man made himself a channel, a vessel for the Great Spirit. Thus he transformed himself from a mere human being into a living companion of God.

This is exactly what we want to do. And according to Cayce, "living an ideal" is a most powerful way to effect the desired change. Jesus used a graphic analogy of how He could be used as an ideal, equating Himself with the bread of life, spiritual life, as the following Bible passage tell us.

The Jews then murmured at him, because he said, 'I am the bread which came down from heaven.' They said, "Is not this Jesus, the son of Joseph, whose father and mother we know? How does he now say, 'I have come down from heaven?'"

Jesus answered them, "Do not murmur among yourselves. No one can come to me unless the Father who sent me draws him; and I will raise him up at the last day. It is written in the prophets, 'And they shall all be taught by God.' Every one who has heard and learned from the Father comes to me. Not that any one has seen the Father except him who is from God; he has seen the Father. Truly, truly, I say to you, he who believes has eternal life. I am the bread of life.

"Your fathers ate the manna in the wilderness, and they died. This is the bread which comes down from heaven, that a man may eat of it and not die. I am the living bread which came down from heaven; if any one eats of this bread, he will live for ever; and the bread which I shall give for the life of the world is my flesh.

The Jews then disputed among themselves, saying, "How can this man give us his flesh to eat?" So Jesus said to them, "Truly, truly, I say to you, unless you eat the flesh of the Son of man and drink his blood, you have no life in you; he who eats my flesh and drinks my blood has eternal life, and I will raise him up at the last day. For my flesh is food indeed, and my blood is drink indeed. He who eats my flesh and drinks my blood abides in me, and I in him. As the living Father sent me, and I live because of the Father, so he who eats me will live because of me. This is the bread which came down from heaven, not such as the fathers ate and died; he who eats this bread will live for ever." This he said in the synagogue, as he taught at Capernaum.

Many of his disciples, when they heard it, said, "This is a hard saying; who can listen to it?" But Jesus, knowing in himself that his disciples murmured at it, said to them, "Do you take offense at this? Then what if you were to see the Son of man ascending where he was before? It is the spirit that gives life, the flesh is of no avail; the words that I have spoken to you are spirit and life. But there are some of you that do not believe." ... And he said, "This is why I told you that no one can come to me unless it is granted him by the Father."

After this many of his disciples drew back and no longer went about with him. Jesus said to the twelve, "Will you also go away?" Simon Peter answered him, "Lord, to whom shall we go? You have the words of eternal life; and we have believed, and have come to know, that you are the Holy One of God. (John 6:41-69)

It's important to realize that the Jews were correct, they did know his father and mother, and they had probably watched him grow up. From all outward appearances this was just a man like other men, and they knew this man. How could he have come down from heaven and become the "bread of life." How could he give them his flesh to eat? From all outward signs this was crazy. Like most of us, they expected Christ to be an external god, not a spirit within a man!

Jesus explains that only someone who has heard God from within will sense the meaning of his words. Such a soul would know the Spirit and could sense Its presence in another. Jesus also quotes the passage that states that all of us will be taught by God Himself (Isaiah 54:13). Why? Because, unlike outward appearances, we are each, from the lowest to the highest, destined to be direct companions to our Creator. No person is before us; each has his or her own birthright to direct contact with the Creator. God will teach each of us – from within.

Even though God will teach each of us directly, Jesus is an Ideal, and if we assimilate this ideal into our systems, we will be transformed. It's like saying, I wanted so much to be a dancer that I ate, drank and slept dancing! Or, as I once heard a famous musical star say, "I imitated my idols to the point that I knew exactly how they would play anything. I became them. Later, as I started to express music as I felt it, I developed my own style. But it was my complete absorption into the music of my idols that helped me develop to a level at which I could express music as I felt it." This is the power of an ideal at work.

Jesus, the embodiment of God in Man, was to be eaten, digested and assimilated as one would do a loaf of bread. In this way the partaker would come to know the true nature of a companion who was one with God, yet living among men in the physical world. Flesh and Spirit would be reconciled. Divine and human would be compatible. Finite would rise again to an awareness and companionship with the Infinite. Life would become continuous; death and separation a thing of the past.

There are two important parts of this concept to keep in mind. First, God will teach us directly, from within. We are not out here alone if we are connected within. Secondly, as we study and apply the elements of our ideal, we begin to assimilate it into our systems (body, mind, heart and soul). This assimilation leads to a transformation that reconciles our contradictions of flesh and spirit, human and divine. God begins to abide with us and we companion with Him.

11. MEDITATION

Developing an ability to enter into deep meditation is a vital tool for achieving higher states of spiritual consciousness and reuniting with our Source. Through meditation a quiet body, a clear mind and an enlivened spirit can rise to the highest state of being that we can perceive, even into the presence of God. Over a period of time, meditation can transform us from mere mortal terrestrial beings to immortal, divine companions with the Whole. It can make our present life on Earth a veritable school for soul growth. Everything can have new meaning.

THE RIGHT HEART

Having the right heart is the first step toward experiencing meaningful, effective meditation. The best techniques won't life a selfish heart into the presence of the Great Spirit. We must free our minds and hearts from things that distract or interfere with our progress. The right thoughts and actions, the right attitudes and emotions throughout the day will do more for our meditation than any technique.

No matter how well we practice these techniques, if we don't hold fast to the right heart and mind, only harm will result. It is the pure in heart that see God (Matt. 5:8), not the skilled in meditative techniques. Here is an appropriate quote from The Secret of the Golden Flower: "He who lacks the right virtue may well find something in it, but heaven will not grant him his Tao. Why not? The right virtue belongs to the Tao as does one wing of a bird to the other: if one is lacking, the other is of no use."

Raising the spiritual forces of our bodies and minds should be done for the right purpose and should be supported by daily actions and thoughts that reflect this purpose. After meditation, it is vital that we apply ourselves to living the Ideal throughout the daily life. It does not matter what type of work we do during the day, only that our attitude and purpose support that which we are seeking when we enter meditation. A person can be an inner city police officer dealing with violence and crime all day and still be able to attune himself to his higher self and the Creator if his actions and thoughts are in accord with his Ideal.

A MEDITATION TECHNIQUE

There are many ways to meditate and as many reasons, but here we will focus on a technique that helps regain spiritual consciousness and union.

Meditation is quieting the physical body and conscious mind, clearing away thoughts and cares of the day, attuning to our inner self and there abiding in a heightened state of awareness and expectancy – quietly listening and waiting for that response from our higher self and the One Spirit. The response comes in many forms and I don't want to limit its possibilities for you. However, I would like to share what others and myself have experienced.

There are specific techniques and exercises for quieting the body and the mind, and arousing our soul. All of these techniques use special activity to achieve inactivity. Since we each have a different perspective, different experiences and are at various levels of development, it's best that we each modify the meditation techniques to suit our own comfort and preference. No one technique works for absolutely everybody, nor for two similar individuals in exactly the same way. The following meditation process is generally very good. It contains some excellent techniques and can be easily modified to suit your personal needs.

That Special Place and Time

Choose a specific place and time to meditate. This helps develop a pattern of response within the body to being in the place for meditation. Regular periods of meditation will accomplish much more than occasional ones. So, select a regular time each day and try not to miss that time. In the beginning you'll generally need only about fifteen minutes for meditation. Later you may want an hour.

Cayce often recommended meditating between 2:00 and 4:00 in the morning. These are good times for meditation. Many great seekers have used this time period for their private awakening and attunement. Cayce said that it is best if you have already slept for some time before awaking to meditation. In this way your body will have had some deep rest and your soul will have had time to awaken from the daily activities to the "nightly wisdom." However, it can be very disruptive to a marriage and a young family! I know. Therefore, keep in mind that the best meditation time is the one you can use regularly. Don't setup 2:00 AM as your meditation time if you can do it or it creates so much turmoil that is becomes a stumbling block rather than a stepping stone! I've had good meditations at 7:00 AM, too.

The important things are a special place and regular time. After you've practiced from some years, you can be more flexible about these requirements, but in the beginning they're very helpful.

Preparation

Begin by cleansing the body with water. Depending on the circumstances, this can be no more than splashing a little water on your face and washing you hands. Then sit or lie in a comfortable position. If you like, you can use one of the Eastern yoga asanas (positions), but I wouldn't suggest forcing yourself into a position that is so unnatural or uncomfortable as to distract you from achieving stillness.

Many people find that stretching exercises before assuming a position make the body more relaxed and ready for being in one position for a long time. I use simple stretches of the spine, limbs and neck. The Edgar Cayce "Head and Neck Exercise" is excellent, here's how it goes: Move the head forward touching the chest with the chin three times, then stretch the head backwards three times, and then to the left three times and the right three times. Then circle the head to the left three times, and then to the right three times. This not only loosens up the neck and shoulder muscles, where a lot of tension forms, but it increases the flow of blood to the head and brain.

Once the exercises are complete, assume the position and become still.

The Breath

Once you are in position, use the Cayce breathing technique to raise the energies of the body: Breathe in through the right nostril and exhale through the mouth three times. While you are breathing in, think "Strength!" Then breathe in through the left nostril and exhale through the right nostril three times. While you do this, think of quietly awakening your inner spirit.

Don't take breathing exercises lightly. Remember how we became physical beings: "The Lord God breathed the breath of life in him and he became a living soul." Breath is life in this dimension and these exercises use that force to raise the level of our life energy and arouse a response our inner being. If you can, let this air be fresh. Often the air in closed rooms is very stale, with little oxygen and many unwanted gases. Open a window if you can.

An Incantation

After you have gotten into position and completed the breathing technique, begin to carry yourself deeper by using an incantation or soft music. Personally, I've found an incantation to be very effective. The sound of your own voice calling forth the spirit within is powerful.

Incantate the sound "Oooommmm" (rhymes with "home") while feeling the sound rise from your lower spiritual centers to the higher ones. This sound is universally effective. On the surface it may appear to be an ancient Sanskrit word of little significance, but it is actually a root sound of much power and purpose. There are many other chants that can be used with good results, but "Om" touches a special cord within.

A variation on the Om incantation is "Aaaarrrreeeeoooommmm." In this incantation the "aaaa" sounds begin in the lower centers and as the sound changes, the energy rises through the centers to the final sound of "mmmm" at the third eye center.

The secret to successful incantation is to think of it as inner sounding. It's not external, like singing. The sounds are meant to resonate inside the body cavities, vibrating the spiritual centers, awakening them to a new level.

The Movement of Energy

At this stage in the meditation, you may begin a technique called "The Circulation of the Light." It is described in detail in the wonderful book, The Secret of the Golden Flower. The circulation of the light combines the cycle of breathing in and out with the rising and falling of the energy along the path from the lower centers to the higher, from the gonads up the spine to the pituitary body in the center of the brain system and behind the middle of the forehead. As one breathes in, the abdomen is drawn in and the energy rises upward along the spinal cord over the top of the head and down into the chambers of the seventh center. Here it meets with the Universal Creative Forces and is transformed into "living water" (Rev. 22:17), and as one exhales it flows down the spinal cord , bathing the centers as it goes. The cycle is continued until there is felt a definite raising of the vibrations of the body.

During the circulation along this path and through the centers, the body may become conscious of distinct vibrations. This is different with each individual, but there are some common sensations. One is a sense of movement within the body. This can result in a feeling that the body is moving back and forth, side to side, in a circular motion, or levitating. It can culminate at the head or reach to areas above the head, like the flame over the disciples' heads when the Holy Spirit was upon them. Don't go looking for this, let it come naturally. And if it never occurs for you, fine – experience the awakening the way it occurs for you. Don't let my words get in the way of your potential.

There may also be feelings of lightness, dizziness and the head being drawn back. Within the spiritual centers one may feel vibrations or pressures. These are indications of an awakening spirit.

The Ideal

After the circulation of the light has been through enough cycles to raise us to a higher vibrational state, like changing water to steam, we should then move our attention away from the technique and let it go on its own again. Our mind should bring forth the highest Ideal we can conceive and focus on the essence of that Ideal, calling all parts of our being to awaken to the Ideal.

When this Ideal is in accord with our superconscious, there may come a flow from "above" to fulfill all that is needed by our minds and our bodies. We may feel stronger, more at one with ourselves and the Universal, a feeling of peace and oneness may come over us. Don't try to possess It. Remain still and silent, in a state of heighten awareness and expectancy, allowing yourself to receive the Spirit without conditions.

Now that I've said this, let me counter it with a seeming contradiction. Opening yourself up to the inner forces requires discernment. Within the spiritual (inner) dimensions are good and evil forces. The Creator has not chosen to destroy the evil ones in hope that they may choose light and goodness eventually. Therefore, you must protect yourself from the free-willed discarnate spirits (inner) realms. The Tars are still among the Wheat. Surround yourself with the protection found in the thought of the Light of Christ, and then discern the spirit to which you attune yourself, and only then open yourself up to the Spirit, as a child would to its mother. We must be guileless as doves and as cunning as serpents to survive. I would add that not only do we need to careful of discarnate spirits, but also of things within our own deep unconscious selves. Within us may be forces of memory and desire that are too powerful for us to handle. Attune yourself to the Spirit, avoid anything less – even though it may appear in sheep's clothing. This is not intended to frighten but to warn and prepare you. Meditation is not dangerous if it is done with proper care and concern, just as driving steel cars next to each other at 65 miles an hour is not dangerous when done with the proper care.

The Deeper Realms

It is difficult to describe the deeper realms of meditation. First of all, there just aren't the words to describe them. It's as though they belong to another dimension altogether and will never be completely describable in three-dimensional terms and concepts. Secondly, I'm not sure we each experience these realms in the same way. It's like trying to discover if we all see the same shade of a color – we may say we do, but do we ever really know unless we each see it through the other's eyes?

I've never met anyone who experienced the deeper realms of meditation every time they meditated. So we shouldn't get too caught up in judging our meditations. Sometimes they'll be great and other times just so-so – at least it will appear that way from the outside. Occasionally, they'll be more than we ever imagined, and we'll go in the strength of that meditation for a very long time!

Very few of us can begin meditating and immediately experience all the wonders of it, but if we don't start we'll certainly not experience them. It is best to begin where you are and waste no time wondering why you aren't experiencing this or that. If you "keep on keeping on", then you're bound to experience all of it.

It is easy to become so involved with the techniques and sensations of meditation that we forget to enter the most vital phase of meditation: Silence. For many of us silence means emptiness or nothingness; to sit in silence would appear to have little value to it. However, the Silence of deep meditation is anything but empty nothingness. It's remarkably revitalizing and rejuvenating; occasionally it's filled with profound sensations, awarenesses and insights, some of which are simply indescribable but make such an impression on us that are changed forever.

Therefore, after you have used the techniques to raise our bodies' vibrations and your consciousness, and aroused your soul from its slumber, become as still and silent as you can. These moments in deep silence will become some of the most valuable moments in your life.

"And when he had opened the seventh seal, there was silence in heaven about the space of half an hour." (Revelation 8:1)

Some Tips

It isn't a good idea to meditate on a full or hungry stomach; it's bad for the digestion and makes it difficult to achieve a deep meditation. If noises are distracting, try using the energy of those noises to raise you to a higher place of consciousness instead of becoming angry or bitter with the outside distractions. If you are caring for children, try to do the best you can to find a reasonably regular period for meditating. If you have a non-supportive spouse, don't flaunt your meditation in front of him or her; try to find a time when he or she won't be affected by your private pursuit. If you are missing the function of one of your endocrine glands because of surgery or malformation, continue to focus on the area where the gland would normally be and you'll get results eventually – remember the centers are spiritual first and physical second, focus on the spiritual. If you find yourself falling asleep during meditation, don't be too concerned about it. Try to maintain a keen sense of quiet awareness for as long as you comfortably can; then let sleep overtake you, but only after you feel you've reached a level of heightened attunement to your Ideal. Sleep frees the soul, and is a natural response to deep meditation. But we are also trying to reunite Spirit and flesh, so the flesh (your outer self) must take part in the attunement.

Many people experience images, sounds, voices and other other stimuli during meditation. These should be a natural response from your higher self after you have reached a keen attunement to your Ideal, and not just intrusions into your meditation. So, control your consciousness in the early stages of a meditation, relaxing your hold on it only after you have the Ideal well in place.

12. CONTACT DREAMS

Dreams are one of the best sources for insight, knowledge and understanding. When the physical body and conscious mind are quiet in sleep, the deeper levels of consciousness can more clearly express themselves. If one learns to remember these expressions and to correctly interpret them, there is no limit to one's knowledge and understanding.

Nothing occurs in one's life that hasn't been foreshadowed in a dream!

How can this be? Even though the predominant level of our consciousness is in the realm of time and space, the deeper levels abide in dimensions beyond time and space and can "see" the road that lies ahead. In fact, these levels of consciousness can also see the road that has been travelled, even back to the beginning of the soul's consciousness. If the conscious mind learns how to listen and understand its deeper levels of consciousness, it can know the forces affecting its life, how best to handle them and what opportunities and perils are ahead. However, the deeper consciousness is not concerned with just the profound or grand things. The everyday needs of life – money, relationships, jobs, diet, physical health, etc. – are all dealt with in dreams. Nothing is too mundane or, for that matter, too grand or holy that one cannot get insight about it from a dream.

When the conscious mind and body are asleep, the subconscious and superconscious use the images, events, people and things of daily physical life to create a somewhat three-dimensional story or message containing information that they need to convey to the conscious level. If the conscious level recalls the dream, studies it, discerns its meaning and, finally, uses the knowledge in its life, then the whole individual begins to grow and fulfill its purpose.

Sometimes the message of a dream is very literal and clear as in this dream.

Dreamed Betty would call tomorrow and I should not be so cool and distant. She will ask me to come visit her and I should go despite my feelings to the contrary.

Betty did call this dreamer just as the dream had predicted, and the dreamer did visit her.

Often the message of a dream has a bizarre element that helps focus the attention of the conscious mind on a particularly important part of the message, as in this dream.

Dreamed I won my preliminary tennis match but as I went over to the stands to be congratulated by everyone my head fell off, and kept falling off. No matter what I did I couldn't keep my head on my shoulders. It was very embarrassing. Finally out of frustration I asked if anyone wanted to go watch Stan play his match. I figured if I could get them to stop looking at me I might be able to keep my head on.

By using this bizarre image the subconscious cleverly warns the conscious self of the potential for losing one's head over an initial victory and becoming too confident and perhaps losing a future match. It even gives him the solution: "Go watch your future opponent play his preliminary match."

In some cases the message of a dream is strongly stated in symbols that deeply affect the conscious self, as in this dream.

I was in the bowels of an old, gray inner-city and on the corner was a fast-food restaurant called, 'Colonel Coffee's Coffins!' When I awoke I did not like the feeling of this dream. It was ominous and I felt like it was serious.

The dreamer's excessive use of coffee to keep him going was causing serious problems within his system, perhaps literally in his bowels. This dream could be interpreted on another level as well. It could pertain to his overall lifestyle of going so fast that he would soon become like a city that had spent its wealth and was decaying.

Interpreting a heavily symbolic dream requires the dreamer of the symbols to identify what those symbols mean to him. The same symbol from two different dreamers can mean two different things. However, there are universal symbols, but even these should be applied individually. When interpreting one's dream, be careful not to prejudice your interpretation by looking for what you want, or by being afraid to find what you hoped for! Be as objective as you can. Pray about the dream. Sometimes it helps to set the dream aside for awhile and return to it later with a second viewing.

When a dream comes from the superconscious mind, its symbolism and imagery is often like that of a vision. I call these Contact Dreams because I feel the dreamer has made contact with his Superconscious and/or the Universal Mind. Here's an example.

I was aboard a large ship with twelve engines. Ten of the engines were working fine, but the eleventh engine was not assembled and the twelfth wasn't even there! When I began to assemble the eleventh engine I heard something behind me. I turned around to see a Jesus glowing so brightly that I could hardly look at Him. He started to move toward me as though He knew me and wanted to greet me with a hug. But I became extremely frightened and fell to the floor, closing my eyes and curling up into a ball as His light engulfed me. At this moment I awoke from the dream as if trying to escape from the scene. I was scared to death and sweating. But once I was awake, I felt upset with myself for not having the courage and trust to be in His presence. Now my bedroom seemed unusually dark and empty. I felt so alone and separated that I vowed never to flee again. Even though I prayed intensely, it took me a long time to get back to sleep.

Dreams from the superconscious can be very intense and filled with meaning, symbology and direct contact with everything an individual holds sacred. Without getting into too much interpretation of this dream, we can see how the dreamer's superconscious portrayed him as a ship with twelve engines (spiritual centers, chakras) and how the conscious self was working on getting all twelve engines running properly. Because of this good work and the dreamer's seeking, he received the opportunity to actually meet the one he sought, Jesus, but it was more than he could bare at this time; certainly it prepared him for a future meeting. The dreamer told me he had only experienced the presence of Jesus once before in a dream and in that case he did not directly see him, just felt he was next to him. He was looking forward to a future meeting and hoped he wouldn't be so scared.

Here is another contact dream but with a little less intensity.

I was walking along the lake at an area where the trees hang over the bank, making it difficult to get by. As I got through the trees I was startled to see a strange man right there in front of me. At first I was very concerned, but he seemed okay. He hadn't noticed me yet. He was fishing. So I carefully continued to walk past him. As I got closed he turned and smiled. I smiled back and managed to ask if he was catching anything. He said, "Yes, but there is one particular fish I've been trying to catch for a very long time and I just can't seem to catch her. Will you help me?" I said I would help him, and then, as though I was helping I just continued to walk by him and along the bank. After I had gotten much farther along, I realized I knew who the man was! It was Jesus. And I knew who the fish was that He wanted me to help Him catch, it was me! When I woke up I felt very good, even excited and ready to go.

Contact dreams are a passage to the spiritual realms and the Spirit of God that can be traveled while still incarnate. Be open to this passage way to the Spirit and the spiritual realms of consciousness.

The Tree of Life

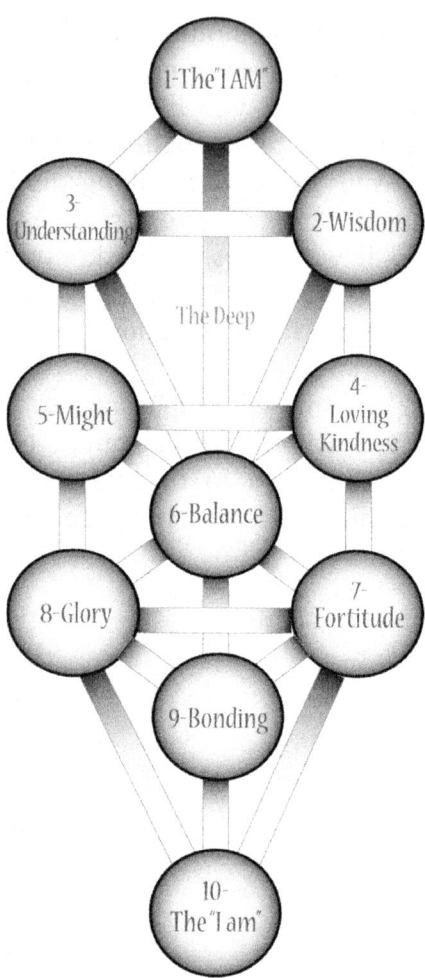

13. A Kabbalah View

Edgar Cayce's teachings contain much akin to Kabbalistic teachings. For example, both teach that life is continuous, there is no death of the soul, and that many dimensions of life extend beyond this physical one. Both teach that all life emanates from the Creator, and that God-consciousness is ever available to us because we are vessels of the Creator's intrinsic nature.

The life force of God, Kabbalah's *Infinite Eternal*, flows from the unseen Creator throughout all of the *observable* creation; and does so in a specific pattern. That pattern is depicted in the Kabbalah Tree of Life. See the illustration on the facing page. This Tree reveals the *Infinite Eternal* through ten *emanations.* The Tree of Life and the ten emanantions are the *mystical* "image of God" (*tselem Elohim*). And since we were initially created in the image of God (as recorded in Genesis 1:26), the emanations and the Tree's pattern reveal how we are constructed and how the Life Energy flows *through us*—the vessels of God. Think of these emanations as *both* beaming Light *from* God and vessels that may *contain* this Light and reflect it back to God.

Like Cayce, Kabbalah conveys a fascinating creation story. As the scientific theory has the Big Bang, Kabbalah teaches that the creation burst forth from the "darkness of the deep" with such intense brilliance, awesome power, and extreme velocity that it broke wide open all the vessels that were to contain the Light of Creation. This was called the "Breaking of the Vessels" (*shevirat ha-keilim*). The vessels were unable to contain the magnitude of the Light—except for the tenth vessel: the "I am" that had been conceived in the image of the Great I AM. Like a mirror, the Little I Am was able to reflect back to the Great I AM the awesome Light of Life. In this way a complete connection was established between the Source of Life and the Vessel of that Life.

Once contained in the heart and mind of the Little I Am, the exploding Light gathered all the shards of the broken vessels and repaired them! Miraculously the image of God was then expressed for all of creation to comprehend. Notice the pathway from the 1st emanation to the 10th and back again? That is the established conduit between God and us.

Like Cayce's teachings, Kabbalah explains that the *original* Little I Am was the *First Being*—what we know today as the Logos, the Word (in the Gospel of John, chapter 1), and the Messiah-Christ. The infinite, unseen creative force of God found its complementary reflection in the First Being. And we are beings *within* the First Being, *within* the Messiah-Christ-Logos-Word. Jesus, speaking as the Christ/Logos, taught: "At that time it will be clear to you that I am in the Father, and you are in me, and I in you." (John 14:20) The Infinite-All of the Creator and the finite beings that we are, actually exist in magical, mysterious oneness! As a result, God-consciousness is always available to us, for within it we exist.

Harmony of Trinities

Before the repair of the broken vessels, chaos reigned. As the Light flowed back to its Source, order was reestablished. The Infinite was now revealed in the finite via *harmony*. According to Kabbalah, this harmonic connection was achieved by "hinging" influences that appear to be opposing one another. When hinged by a third influence the opposites form a harmonious trinity. Notice the triangles of *triads* in this illustration.

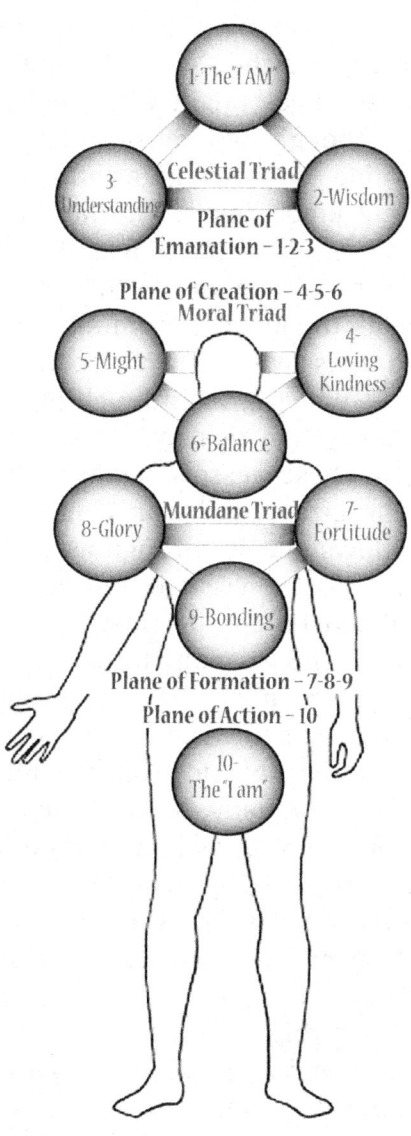

For example, looking at the illustration you see that Understanding (Hebrew *tebunah*) is hinged to Wisdom (*chokmah*) by the Great I AM, thus bringing the developmental discernment that leads to Understanding in harmony with the innate condition of Wisdom. This forms the Celestial Triad. Next you'll see how Balance hinges Might with Loving-kindness, indicating that though we must be strong within ourselves, shielded from negative influences we also must be lovingly kind. This is the Moral Triad. And finally you'll see that Bonding hinges the Glory of our inborn Godly nature with the Fortitude (endurance) necessary to walk the journey from immature souls to eternal companions with our Creator. This is the Mundane Triad—which gives a much higher purpose to our mundane life than we may realize.

With all of these vessels repaired, in harmony, illuminated, energized, and consciously awakened, Light and Life flows evenly throughout the creation— from the Creator to the created and back again. You see, from a Kabbalistic perspective, "sin" is when the flow is broken, i.e., the harmony lost. To restore health and wellbeing, reunion of the energy between the vessel of life and the source of life must be achieved. By understanding this holistic principle and applying it in our lives, we gradually become more heavenly, more eternal—less temporary, less materialistic, and less constrained by physical reality and self-centeredness. As our consciousness expands and our heavenly heart grows, the Light of Life flows through us with strength and vigor, further illuminating our minds and enlivening our hearts. Life, love, and relationships are in *harmony*. When we apply these principles properly in our daily lives, we naturally become better people: better friends, neighbors, spouses, and parents. We gain a rare *patience* that changes the very dynamic of physical life and imbues us with our Creator's Light.

Planes of Existence

Many of us have come to understand the differences in states of consciousness and dimensions of life; the difference between a materialistic mind with its focus on physical reality, and its opposite, an *enlightened* mind—resulting in feelings beyond self-centeredness, self-gratification, and self-exaltation. When we are enlightened, we have musical appreciation, quality love relationships, and awareness and care beyond our own little world. We comprehend the laws governing the universe, while others just live in it, not aware of what is involved. Today we grasp the concept of paradigms, archetypes, mental constructs, and emotional patterns. We can appreciate theoretical frameworks which point to unseen influences upon reality.

Now we might quickly use the term *states of consciousness* but we need to retain some of the qualities of this world, for Cayce's readings warn that even in higher dimensions where the physical body does not exist, there are magnetic-like forces that create a vessel-like field for each soul-mind—a type of nonphysical "body." Cayce teaches that the physical plane is not so much different than the other planes; it is a shadow of them. When in the other planes our individualness is not as encased as it is in a physical body, because our *individual consciousness* can expand into infinity and back again at will! We can be both finite and infinite. This is achieved through our enlightened mind. And here's the exciting news: this can be experienced right here, right now! We don't have to physically die to experience all of the planes of life because our enlightened mind does the "traveling."

Let's examine more closely Kabbalah's planes where personal consciousnesses with body-like orbs of beingness may experience multi-dimensional life—something we will eventually do forever.

Here are the planes that are common to most Kabbalistic texts. In the illustration on page 173 you'll notice how they correlate with the Triads, except for the lowest plane, which is where you and I live today!

1. Plane of Emanation (*Olam Atzilut*)

The central realm of existence is the Plane of Emanation. It is both the origin and destiny of the sons and daughters of God. On this plane the Visible Expressed Life unites with the Hidden Source of Life. Here we may know oneness with the *Infinite Eternal*. This is the plane of the Divine Personae (*partzufim*) and the Brilliant Light. Here is the realm of the Infinite, the Omnipotent, All-knowing, Universal Mind and Spirit. All of creation is in this plane but in its *uncontaminated* state, *pure* as the moment in which it was divinely conceived. The perfection of this realm is not affected by what goes on in the lower realms. Cayce agrees, stating that our perfect, in-the-image-of-God self, has not been contaminated by anything. To perceive this realm is to be in ecstasy, bliss, nirvana, samadhi, and all the other terms humans have used to describe the "peace that passes understanding," the contentment that brings enduring happiness.

2. Plane of Creation (*Olam Briah*)

The *Light* of Creation gave life to the Plane of Creation. That which came out of "the deep" expresses its qualities in this plane (See the location of "The Deep" in the illustration on page 170). Here are the Creative Forces. This is the plane of the archangels and divine souls (*neshamot mekoriyyah*). The life essence of the Creator permeates this realm, giving goodness to all. In the first plane the ten emanations of God are called Lights; in this plane they are called *Spirits*—and are divine beings. A portion of us exists on this plane. Here is the domain of First Being, within which we have our beingness, but at a divine level.

3. Plane of Formation (*Olam Yetzirah*)

The third plane is the Plane of Formation. Here the unseen essences take form, in the sense of fields of unique energy and consciousness, not bodies. This is the plane of angels and the *Orphanim* ("Never-sleeping Watchers/Guardians"). Here we find the laws that shape the patterns of creation and form the seven heavens, seven ages, seven chakras (though not yet physical), and so on. Here we find the higher element of ether, or *akasha* in Sanskrit; this is the most subtle and expansive of the five elements (earth, water, fire, air, and ether). Every thought, word, and action of every soul makes an impression upon the akasha, and records its *Book of Remembrance*.

4. Plane of Action (*Olam Asiyah*)

The fourth plane is the Plane of Action. It is the physical realm where the created souls engage their wills to do as they desire and experience the reaction —which we know to be karma: "What goes around, comes around." In this realm we find the physical universe, particularly our galaxy. This plane is also called the "Elemental Plane of Substance." At all times in this plane there are Light Forces struggling against dark influences—each attempting to possess the hearts and minds of the developing souls.

5. Plane of Repairing and Perfecting (*Tikkun Olam*)

This brings us to the forces of "Repairing and Perfecting Plane." In Lurianic Kabbalah there is this fifth plane. Remember the vessels that shattered because they could not contain and reflect the original Light of God? Well their shards became sparks of light *trapped* in the material world. Contemplative prayer releases the sparks and allows them to flow to God's Light, thus repairing and restoring God's Essence throughout. Like Cayce, the Kabbalah encourages "contemplative prayer," which we would consider to be prayer mingled with meditative receptivity to the Divine Light.

Edgar Cayce and the Planes

Cayce's teachings often address planes. In one reading he confirms the Kabbalah's four planes and then in another reading he lists five, as found in Lurianic Kabbalah. But Cayce also indicates that there are now more planes!

"In most every group that has approached such subjects, *planes* are rarely understood. They are accounted as to the first, second, third, fourth, fifth plane; yet we find *these* [are] only ... the beginnings of the activities of those influences of the souls of men." (EC 507-2) He explains: "In flesh must the entity manifest and make the will one with the God ... and as such development reaches that plane wherein the development may pass into other spheres and systems, of which our solar system is only a small part; then ... the entity must develop in that sphere until it (the entity) has reached that stage wherein it may manifest through the *spiritual planes*." (EC 900-25)

According to Cayce's teachings our soul must progress through all the planes to become completely conscious of and companionable to our Creator.

In one reading (900-355) Cayce correlates "planes of conditions" with "phases of consciousness": growth and transformation occur within the *mind* as we progress through various phases of awareness and understanding. The other planes are not reached by *traveling* to them but by developing *awareness* of them. Such awareness may not be fully in our conscious mind except by an *intuitive knowing* that results from our *enlightened* mind. And contemplative prayer is the means.

Each soul sojourns in nonphysical realms or planes and incarnates into the physical world for the same duel purpose of enlightening the mind and enlivening the heart. Each of us eventually becomes *companionable* to our Creator, who loves us and longs for our conscious companionship, sharing the gift of Life with us.

Reincarnation & Karma

14. A Gnostic View

In Gnosticism the "Woman of the Light" is legendary Sophia; her Greek name means *Wisdom*. Some of the richest legends of battles between the Light and the Dark are battles by women, and Sophia's is a classic. She carries the epithet of "Wisdom from Above" (*he ano Sophia*). But she is also a female spirit (*he kato Sophia*). In her ideal essence she is, as were the Mayan *Xquic* (pronounced *Sh-queek*) and Egyptian *Isis*, the "Lightsome Mother" (*he Meter he Photeine*).

There are many tales about Sophia; one story tells how her love for "Unknown God" (*hagnostos theos*) drove her to seek to know him directly and to comprehend his greatness. However, such a realization would have ultimately meant the evaporation of her very being into the immensity of his infinite, un-individuated nature – what is called, "the Bliss of Oblivion." It would be like entering an infinite abyss. Fortunately, a "Boundary Spirit" saved her from oblivion. Boundary Spirits are stationed throughout the cosmos to guide, guard, and help those seeking contact with the Infinite, Un-differentiated Essence from which all life emanates – what Kabbalah calls "the Deep."

After the creation began, Sophia perceived that chaos would result as multiplicity overwhelmed oneness and endless layers of subsequent creations spun on and on and on from the original. To bring order to the chaos, she created the material universe and specifically our Solar System (*Hebdomad*), which is known as "the Seven Heavens." She is the "Mother of the Seven Heavens."

It is said that her concern over the chaos of multiplicity caused her to hurry back into the depths of Unknown God without losing herself in his immensity. This contact with him produced an offspring! But, as all good legends go, she still maintained her virginal goddess condition (Did you expect any less?). This is so like the Egyptian goddess Isis, who sought to conceive a messiah to help her save the lost souls on earth, and she did so without sexual intercourse with a mere man or even a god. However, unlike Isis, who immaculately conceived the messiah god Horus, Sophia projected a "formless substance," which some believe was the Fifth Element – not one of the four elements: earth, water, fire, and air. Classic teachings as well as the Edgar Cayce teachings consider *ether* to be the fifth element, and associate it with the Akashic Records, as does Hinduism. (Just a side note: science currently considers *plasma* (electrified particles, not the blood component) to be the the *fourth state of matter*, thus solid, liquid, gas, and plasma.)

In a story found in the *Pistis Sophia* (Chapter XXIX), Sophia originally dwelt in the "Highest Heaven," but she was seduced by a demon (a male demon of course!). The demon used a ray of light to deceive her. She mistook the light as an emanation from God. She pursued this light and it led into the "Realm of Chaos" below the "Twelve Lights." It was darkness and she was captured and imprisoned by the Dark Forces.

After Sophia had fallen from the Highest Heaven and become captive in matter, Unknown God, who loved her, emanated two new Lights in order to save her. Now this may sound strange, but the Gnostic legend identifies these two new Lights as Christ (the Logos or "Word," as in the opening of John's Gospel) and the Holy Spirit. Christ and the Holy Spirit take hold of Sophia's "formless substance" and give it essence and form, whereupon Sophia tries to rise again to Unknown God, but she cannot fully make it from where she is. To help her, Unknown God emanates "the Savior," who must come down into the realms of matter and unite himself with the man Jesus, the son of an enlightened, virgin woman in Nazareth named Mary! (I know, it's amazing!) The Savior's light illuminates predisposed souls moving down the stream of time and space, igniting the truth that lies dormant within the inner recesses of their being. Cayce's teachings agree, stating: "The Christ-Consciousness is an awareness within each soul, imprinted on the mind and *waiting to be awakened* by the will, of the soul's oneness with God." (EC 5749-14, my italics)

This Savior is not a man, but a Light that entered the man, Jesus, and manifested through him for all to see. The Savior is the Holy Spirit that was *in* Jesus, rather than the man Jesus. A distinction that Cayce's teachings also make: "Jesus is the man; Christ is the spirit." (EC 262-15)

In the legend of Sophia, she becomes the "Bride of Christ," and is saved from the deception of the Dark Forces, which can be so subtle as to appear to be the Light. As Jesus warned, "The Kingdom of God doesn't come with observation; neither will they say, 'Look, here!' or 'Look, there!' for behold, the Kingdom of God is within you." (Luke 17:20-21) Ultimately Christ in this legend is the "Bridegroom" and Sophia (*Wisdom*) is the Bride. John the Baptist uses this same imagery as he explains his role and that of the one who is coming after him: "No one can receive anything except what is given him from heaven. You yourselves bear me witness that I said, I am not the Christ, but I have been sent before him. He who has the bride is the bridegroom; but the friend of the bridegroom, who stands and hears him, rejoices greatly at the bridegroom's voice; therefore this joy of mine is now full." (John 3:27-29, my italics)

Here is a curious passage from the Bible that complements the Gnostic story of our initial wisdom, perfection, and subsequent fall from that grace.

> "You were the signet of perfection, full of wisdom and perfect in beauty. You were in Eden, the garden of God; every precious stone was your covering ... and wrought in gold were your settings and your engravings. On the day that you were created they were prepared for you. With an anointed guardian cherub I placed you there. You were on the holy mountain of God, in the midst of the stones of fire you walked. You were blameless in your ways from the day you were created, until iniquity was found in you."
> –Ezekiel 28:12-15

15. Hindu Perspectives

As most all if us know, the Eastern world has always accepted reincarnation and karma as facts of life, of the life of the spiritual, soul part of our being. Before we actually get into the teachings we have to have a basic understanding of the Hindu Trinity. Yes, like Christianity's Father, Son, and Holy Spirit, Hinduism has a triune perspective on God's three qualities. Trinity is not an expression of multiple gods but an attempt to render the infinite, one God in three understandable roles. These three are meant to help our three dimensional nature better comprehend the infinite, eternal God and our relationship with God.

In Hinduism, the Trinity is Brahma, Vishnu, and Shiva. Brahma is the creator; Vishnu, the preserver; and Shiva, the destroyer of ignorance and illusions. Brahma put its eternal spirit into all of the creation. The eternal spirit takes no form but is expressed by the Life Forced or Life Essence in any form. The individual spirit of a creation is always connected to the one, omnipresent eternal Creator (Brahma). Brahma is depicted with four heads facing in the cardinal directions, and four hands—one holding a water bottle (symbol of life), another holding prayer beads (symbol of devotion), another the Vedas (symbol of knowledge), and one hand holding a creation tool (*sruva*, a symbol of his role as creator).

Vishnu, the second part of the Trinity, is depicted with one head, which is surrounded by several (often seven) flared cobra heads. In his four hands are a conch shell, indicating the spread of the divine sound OM; a spinning disk of light representing a chakra or spiritual center within the body and the wheel of time; a lotus, indicating enlightenment; and the mace of lordship, indicating his role.

Shiva, the third portion of the triune Godhead, is most often depicted as being in meditation with the water of life coming out of his topknot and running upward and back to a high mountain, representing the source of original life from which we all came. A third eye on his forehead conveys his deeper sight. His eyes half closed, reveal his inner vision. And his body covered in ashes symbolizes life beyond death. A moon crescent is seen near his head, and the radiant sun surrounds his head like a halo, both revealing his ability to be in the source of all light (the sun) and to reflect that light when in darkness (the moon).

The Wheel of Rebirth

"This vast universe is a wheel. Upon it are all creatures that are subject to birth, death, and rebirth. Round and round it turns, and never stops. It is the wheel of Brahman. As long as the individual self thinks it is separate from Brahman [the Creator portion of the Trinity], it revolves upon the wheel in bondage to the laws of birth, death, and rebirth. But when through the grace of Brahma it realizes its identity with him, it revolves upon the wheel no longer. It achieves immortality."–Svetasvatara Upanishad (Prabhavananda), 118

Bhagavad Gita

"15:7 An eternal portion of Myself, having become a living soul in a world of living beings, draws to itself the five senses, with the mind for the sixth, which

abide in *Prakriti* [fundamental substrate of matter]. "15:8 When the lord acquires a body, and when he leaves it, he takes these with him and goes on his way, as the wind carries away the scents from their places.
"15:9 Presiding over the ear and eye, the organs of touch, taste, and smell, and also over the mind, he experiences sense-objects.
"15:10 The deluded do not perceive him when he departs from the body or dwells in it, when he experiences objects or is united with the *gunas* [qualities: These three gunas are called: *sattva* (goodness, constructive, harmonious), *rajas* (passion, active, confused), and *tamas* (darkness, destructive, chaotic)]; but they who have the eye of wisdom perceive him."

Karma: The Law of Action

"According to the doctrine of karma, for every morally determinate thought, word, or action, there will be corresponding karmic compensation, if not in this life, then in some future life. As a man sows, so shall he reap." –K. L. Sheshagiri Rao, in *Pappu*, 23

"He, as the Self, resides in all forms, but is veiled by ignorance... At death he is born again, and the circumstances of his new life are determined by his past deeds and by the habits he has formed." –Kaivalya Upanishad (Prabhavananda), 115

Patanjali wrote in *Yoga Sutras*: 2:14. "Experiences of pleasure and of pain are the results of merit and demerit, respectively."

The Law of Desire

"Others, however, say that a person consists of desires. As is his desire, so is his will; as is his will, so is the deed he does, whatever deed he does, that he attains." –Brhad-aranyaka Upanisad (Radhakrishnan), IV.4.5

"The desires we get are actually *samskaras* (impulses). They are formed in this way: 1. Having union with an object [including a person], possessing it. 2. The object is not present, but stays in the mind. 3. A craving for the object is created. 4. The craving makes a print on the mind which remains after death (*samskara*, a longing). Desire is actually the third stage [of influences to reincarnate]. We don't feel the first two stages, they are too subtle. Samskaras (impulses) recreate desires in the next birth automatically. A person can get the desire to steal though brought up in a good family. He himself can't understand why he desires it. These desires develop more when they are fulfilled. Desires can be overcome by controlling them; we have to put a limit on desires." –Baba Hari Dass, 116

"The karmic law requires that every human wish find ultimate fulfillment. Nonspiritual desires are thus the chain that binds man to the reincarnational wheel. –Paramahansa Yogananda, 360 Samskaras

Patanjali wrote (2:12-13): "A man's latent tendencies have been created by his past thoughts and actions. These tendencies will bear fruits, both in this life and in lives to come. So long as the cause exists, it will bear fruits – such as rebirth, a long or short life, and the experiences of pleasure and of pain."

"Every action that you do produces a two-fold effect. It produces an impression in your mind and when you die you carry the Samskara (impulse) in the *Karmashaya* (consequences) or receptacle of works in your subconscious mind. It produces an impression on the world or Akashic records." –Swami Sivananda (1), 95

"If you eat a mango, if you do any kind of work, it produces an impression in the subconscious mind or Chitta. This impression is called Samskara or tendency.

Whatever you see, hear, feel, smell or taste causes Samskaras (impulses or tendencies). The acts of breathing, thinking, feeling and willing produce impressions. These impressions are indestructible. They can only be fried in toto by *Asamprajnata Samadhi* (ecstasy of understanding). Man is a bundle of Samskaras. Man is a bundle of impressions. It is these Samskaras that bring a man again and again to this physical plane. They are the cause for rebirths. These Samskaras assume the form of very big waves through memory, internal or external stimulus." –Swami Sivananda (1), 95

"The impulse behind most human actions insofar as man is a psychophysical being comes from what are called *samskaras* (subliminal and latent tendencies) and *vasanas* (desires rooted in the psyche at an unconscious level but their force is also consciously felt). Each human being is born with a certain configuration of these samskaras and vasanas (their precise nature determined by action in a previous life) and these, felt as attraction towards some things and aversion towards others, act as driving forces behind our actions, insofar as we act out the dharma of our being as part of nature." –Pratima Bowes, in Pappu, 175

"Karma is divided into four categories: 1. *sanchita karma*, or the accumulated past actions; 2. *prarabdha karma*, or that part of past-action karma which results in this present birth and is known as predestination; 3. *kriyamana karma*, or present willful actions, or free will; and 4. *agami karma*, or the immediate results caused by our present actions." –Sant Keshavadas, 8

The Experience of Death

"The point of his heart becomes lighted up and by that light the self departs either through the eye or the head or through other apertures of the body. And when he thus departs, life departs after him. And when life thus departs, all vital breaths depart after it. He becomes one with intelligence. What has intelligence departs with him. His knowledge and his work take hold of him as also his past experience. Just as a leech (or caterpillar) when it has come to the end of a blade of grass, after having made another approach (to another blade), draws itself together towards it, so does this self, after having thrown away the body, and dispelled ignorance, after having another approach (to another body) draws itself together (for making the transition to another body). And as a goldsmith, taking a piece of gold turns it into another, newer and more beautiful shape, even so does this self, after having thrown away this body and dispelled its ignorance, make unto himself another, new and more beautiful shape like that of the fathers or of the *gandharvas* (heavenly beings), or of the gods or of Praja-pati (creation deities) or of Brahma (the Creator) or of other beings." –Brhad-aranyaka Upanisad (Radha-krishnan), IV.4.2

"There are two states for man: the state in this world, and the state in the next. There is also a third state, the state intermediate between these two, which can be likened to dream. While in the intermediate state, and man experiences both the other states, that in this world and that in the next; and the manner thereof is as follows: When he dies, he lives only in the subtle body, on which are left the impressions of his past deeds, and of these impressions he is aware, illumined as they are by the pure light of the Self. Thus it is that in the intermediate state he experiences the first state, or that of life in the world. Again, while in the intermediate state, he foresees both the evils and the blessings that will yet come to him, as these are determined by his conduct, good or bad, upon the earth, and by the character in which this conduct has resulted. Thus it is that in the intermediate state he experiences the second state, or that of life in the world to come. In the intermediate state there are no real chariots, nor horses, nor roads; but by the light of the Self he creates [like a dream] chariots and horses and roads. There are no real blessings, nor joys, nor pleasures; but he creates blessings and joys and pleasures. There are no real ponds, nor lakes, nor rivers; but he creates ponds and lakes and rivers. He is the creator of all these out of the impression left by his past deeds." –Brihadaranyaka Upanishad (Prabhavananda), 105

Experiences After Death

"Some say that those who after death pass into the path of light are not reborn, whereas those who after death take the path of darkness are reborn after they have enjoyed the fruits of karma in their subtle bodies." –Ramana Maharshi, 198

Interestingly, Edgar Cayce actually gave 18 people the message that this was their last incarnation. They would be reincarnating again – unless of course the used their free wills to do so. But it was no longer their karmic cycle to do so.

The Path of the Gods

On this there are the following verses: "The narrow ancient path which stretches far away, has been touched (found) by me, has been realized by me. By it, the wise, the knowers of Brahman go up to the heavenly world after the fall of the body, being freed (even while living). That path was found by a *Brahmana* (Hindu religious texts) and by it goes the knower of Brahman, the doer of right and the shining one." –Brhad-aranyaka Upanisad (Radhakrishnan), IV. 4.8-9

"Verily, when a person departs from this world, he goes to the air. It opens out there for him like the hole of a chariot wheel. Through that he goes upwards. He goes to the sun. It opens out for him like the hole of a *lambara* [drum]. Through that he goes upwards. He reaches the moon. It opens out there for him like the hole of a drum. Through that he goes upwards. He goes to the world free from grief, free from snow. There he dwells eternal years." –Brhad-aranyaka Upanisad (Radhakrishnan), V.10.1

This teaching continues: "Then when he dies, They carry him to (be offered in) fire. His fire itself becomes the fire, fuel the fuel, smoke the smoke, flame the flame, coals the coals, sparks the sparks. In this fire the gods offer a person. Out of this offering the person, having the color of light, arises. Those who know this as such and those too who meditate with faith in the forest on the truth, pass into the light, from the light into the day, from the day into the half-month of the waxing moon, from the half-month of the waxing moon into the six months during which the sun travels northward, from these months into the world of the gods, from the world of the gods to the sun, from the sun into the lightning (fire). Then a person consisting (born) of mind goes to those regions of lightning and leads them to the worlds of Brahman. In these worlds of Brahma they live for long periods. Of these there is no return." –Brhad-aranyaka Upanisad (Radhakrishnan), VI.2.13-15

It continues: "So those who know this, and those who in the forest meditate on faith as austerity (or with faith and austerity [austerity here means "without desires or impulses"]) go to light and from light to day, from day to the bright half of the month (of the waxing moon), from the bright half of the month to those six months during which the sun moves northward. From these months to the year, from the year to the sun, from the sun to the moon, from the moon to the lightning. There, there is a person who is non-human. He leads them on to Brahma. This is the path leading to the gods. – Chandogya Upanisad (Radhakrishnan), V.9.1-2

Again it is helpful here to keep in mind that even Jesus Christ taught that we are "gods" (John 10:34), children of the One God. He is referring to Psalm 82:6: "You are gods, And all of you sons [and daughters] of the Most High." And the ancient Egyptians called us "godlings" of the Great God.

Back to the Hindu text: "Now, the self is the bridge, the (separating) boundary for keeping these worlds apart. Over that bridge day and night do not cross, nor old age nor death, nor sorrow, nor well-doing nor ill-doing. All evils turn back from it for the Brahma-world is freed from evil. Therefore, verily, on crossing that bridge, if one is blind he becomes no longer blind, if wounded he becomes no longer wounded, if afflicted he becomes no longer afflicted. Therefore, verily, on crossing that bridge, night appears even as day for that Brahma-world is ever-illumined." –Chandogya Upanisad (Radhakrishnan), VIII.4.1-3

The Crown Chakra (Fontanelle, or "Soft Spot")

"It is necessary that the subtle forces and the *manas* (supernatural forces) which contain the consciousness of the dying man should come out of the top of the head through a fissure called Brahma's hole, which plays a great part in Asian anatomy. If the human being disengages himself thus, says the tradition, he retains a clear consciousness of his state, and, above all, at a given moment (twenty to twenty-five minutes after apparent death), experiences the ecstatic state which is an absolute reproduction of the *samadhi* (ecstasy) of the yogi, a state which permits him to realize his union with the Divine. This is an opportunity open to every human being who dies, but unfortunately very few become aware of this possibility." –Jean Marques-Riviere, *Mantrik Yoga*, 170.

The Mind-Body Problem

"The theory of karma and rebirth would seem to hold that the unique qualities of our mental character (talents, likes and dislikes, emotional tendencies, etc.) carry over from one birth to the next. This is possible because these tendencies reside in the subtle body (*linga sharira*) or one of the still subtler levels contained within it. This is a difficult conclusion to understand in light of our modern knowledge of the brain. Now, we certainly don't understand how the brain works in detail. However, we do know how to mess the brain up in a great variety of different ways. Accidents, drugs, surgery, shock treatments, strokes and tumors do a very efficient job of disorganizing various aspects of the brain. The really interesting fact is that none of those qualities that comprise our mental character is immune from such accidents. We can lose our memory, our talents, the normal emotional tone of our personality, and our likes and dislikes because of various cerebral accidents and injuries. And of course, we can lose all our faculties as well, such as the ability to reason, to form speech, to control our bodies, etc. Now, if the subtle body is sufficient to support the existence of a mental life, including all our faculties and all the unique qualities of our mental character, then why is the brain also necessary, and why cannot these mental qualities continue when the brain is damaged? One answer I can think of is that, once the subtle body enters a physical body, it somehow becomes limited by that physical body. It is as if you were sitting buckled in at the driver's seat of a car. If the engine breaks down, you can't go anywhere without unbuckling the seatbelt, opening the door, and leaving the car. The engine could correspond to any of our brain functions. The departure from the car would be the equivalent of dying or having an out of body experience. Similarly, the *Katha Upanisad* says: 'Know the Self as the lord of the chariot and the body as, verily, the chariot, know the intellect as the charioteer and the mind as, verily, the reigns.'" –Katha Upanisad (Radhakrishnan), I.3.3

It is amazing how much knowledge about reincarnation and karma, death and rebirth, has been taught, studied, and explained in various ways in the Eastern cultures, particularly by the ancient Hindus.

Edgar Cayce on Grace versus Karma

"As [one] sets itself to accomplish that which is of a creative influence ... no longer is the entity under the law of cause and effect or karma, but rather in grace." (EC 2800-2)

"Do that which is good, for there has been given in the consciousness of all the Fruits of the Spirit: Fellowship, kindness, gentleness, patience, long-suffering, love; these be the Fruits of the Spirit. Against such there is no law. Doubt, fear, avarice, greed, selfishness, self-will; these are the fruits of the evil forces. Against such there is a law. Self-preservation, then, should be in the fruits of the spirit, as you seek through any channel to know more of the path from life to life; from good to good; from death unto life, from evil unto good. Seek and you shall find. Meditate on the Fruits of the Spirit in the inner secrets of the consciousness, and the cells in the body become aware of the awakening of the life in their activity through the body. In the mind, the cells of the mind become aware of the life in the Spirit. The spirit of life makes not afraid. Then, know the way; for those that seek may find." (EC 5752-3)

CPSIA information can be obtained
at www.ICGtesting.com
Printed in the USA
FSOW03n1129060916
24650FS